To the reader

Probably, this book has come to you in a peculiar way, the law of the cause; when you finish reading it, you are free to do what you please with it; if you consider it has served you well, send thoughts of gratitude and love to whom brought it into your hands.

This is just a talk with death, something that you might even be afraid to think about, someday, certainly, you will have to face. It will be up to you to become a sower of life…

Once you've finished reading it, if you consider the book did nothing for you, we kindly ask you to leave it somewhere; there is no doubt it will attract a soul that will value it. If you get to the end, and you wish to become a sower of life, such act will transcend in you incarnations.

At the end of the path of life, when you are face to face with death, there shall be a judgment, where the most important thing is: What did you not do in life, having had the chance to do it?

Omar Hejeile Ch.

AUTHOR
Omar Hejeile Ch.

Editorial Wicca rescues the immeasurable power of human beings and nature; a power everyone possesses, feels, and perceives, but few know. By means of texts, and radio programs, we invite without imposing a truth or a concept, so each one who feels the calling from within, who discovers the magic of dreams, and wishes to obtain the knowledge, thus, the transformation of their life can reach the center of **happiness.**

The old religion has been reborn…
and it is in your hands.

WICCA SCHOOL OF MAGIC

The old religion based on the magical knowledge, of ancient cultures lost in time, escaped from the world of the hyperboreans, the harmony between man and nature are reborn like the phoenix.

Wicca, term that comes from Wise, Wizard; means "The trade of the wise", "The artisans of wisdom". During millennia of persecution, the ancient documents of the old religion remained hidden awaiting for the proper moment to be reborn; now, Wicca, recovers several of the old knowledge about the influence of the moon, the sun, the great Sabbats, the secret power of enchantments and spells, the art of incantations, the infinite magical world of plants, and the secret of the stars.

More information in:

www.ofiuco.com
www.radiokronos.com
www.wiccausa.com

© 2022
Author: Omar Hejeile Ch.

Copyrights

Tittle: Talks with Death, The Value of Life

ISBN: 979-837-0575-67-9

Editorial Seal: WICCA E.U. (978-958-8391)

ENCYCLOPEDIA: "Universe of Magic"

Design and Layout: Mario Sánchez C.

No part of this publication, including the cover art, may be reproduced, stored or transmitted in any way by no means, be it electrical, chemical, mechanical, optical, recording, photocopying or television space, press, radio, internet without prior permission of the publisher.

Based on copyright, the images used to recreate are free to use those inside the book.

www.wiccausa.com

(Copyright 2022, All Rights Reserved EDITORIAL WICCA)

TALKS CON LA DEATH

THE VALUE OF LIFE

CHARLAS CON LA MUERTE

מדבר עם המוות

וויקה

TALKS WITH DEATH

It is the short phrase that lets you know, that life has ended; everything has ended, the world of opportunities, the everlasting source of options and opportunities, are all drops that evaporate in the deserted sands of a tomorrow that shall never exist again.

Everything has ended, life has extinguished, but... In the same and mournful instant... Another life... Another fantastic experience... Has begun.

...You are about to enter an unknown universe; you are about to open the door to the boundaries of life and enter the strange, abysmal, and sinister mazes of death.

A parallel world where life takes force and the spirit is freed from earthly chains; the world of death, so empty and strange, where perpetual souls cry out for just one more second of life, but the agonic silence of the departure, the distant arcane of the lived, in pilgrim memories of dawns already withered, lie asleep in the impassable yesterday.

Decorated graves, cadavers trapped in the soft gauzes that sing to sleep the cold petrified skeletons in their boxes, dark caves, doorways to eternity where the empty sockets watch without looking at the wasted life or the glory achieved before the inevitable departure.

Everything happens in the time without time, just an instant separates the fragile abyss between life and death, no matter how it comes, the end is the same, a soft gloom wraps the senses, a nice fog holds the soul, feelings scape and the illusions depart, everything vanishes forever in the nothing. The story begins... As an omen of what will happen tomorrow, the postponed appointment shall take place without knowing when or where it shall take place, but one day, one hour, one minute, one second, shall be the last second to exist.

Opened eyes see without seeing, the body remains inert, the crimson cause of life stops its walk, the air source of sighs has exhausted the senses, the cold of the nothing appears with its black shroud and the beneficial death liberates the soul.

Everything happens in the time with no time, like an eternal melody life escapes, it is there, where one contemplates for an instant, with a fleeting glance, the second that marks, the end of the day.

Celestial lights, angelical gates, enchanted landscapes overwhelm the spirit with the warmth of a feeling that captivates the senses, there is no smell, there is no moaning, there is no fear, there is nothing, just that strange inexplicable sensation of freedom, profound love and peace.

CHARLAS CON LA MUERTE

מדבר עם המוות

...The soul shivers for being outside of the body, the moment of death is an instant, no matter how it happens, accident, disease, it is all the same; death, in it self, can't be felt, most of the people doesn't even realize they are dead, consciousness remains intact, just when matter doesn't exist it is when reality is understood, that this life has ceased to exist, forever, in the profound universe of the nothing.

The sudden darkness, the feeling of emptiness, all the senses are sharpened, all emotions are calmed, everything disappears, physical pain doesn't exist; in an instant, everything is different, the spirit escapes like a fog that flows, that is outside in a fantastic experience, the soul is freed.

For a time without time, the inert body is contemplated, the mind remains alive maintaining the identity and the memories, but there is no sacred union between this world and the spirit, that bond has been broken forever.

The material world is contemplated, as the last flash, all that in life was part of existence, a body, objects, treasures, memories, wealth, everything vanishes in the nothing.

וויקה

Nothing can be felt, nothing can be touched, nothing really exists, all the things that were once part of the material life, are now unreachable, the body thru which the spirit coexisted has already stopped being part of the experience, it now is an abandoned jail, something grotesque, a prison that is slowly extinguished and forever nothing.

One feels gratitude and fear, a lot of fear, seeing the cadaveric and inert body, the eyes without shine, the perpetual rigidity, and the pale and macabre demeanor of death. The last vision of the material world, there is no pain… No sorrow… The initial shock slowly begins to produce an indescribable calm. The emotions harmonize; the transition to the afterlife is, in some way pleasant, a calm and serenity that comes before the worst of the storms of the soul.

…Everything has vanished, a strange fog slowly flowed from every place, death floated huddled, there is no body, nothing, you are just there, it is a strange feeling, it is a live thought, without emotions, without senses, without nothing… but there, there is the whole life, you are fused with everything there is, if it really is.

CHARLAS CON LA MUERTE

מדבר עם המוות

OMAR HEJEILE CH.

מדבר עם המוות

ויקה

TALKS WITH DEATH

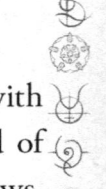

Few times in life one has the opportunity to talk with death, while it will happen someday, in the road of existence it remains huddled in the world of shadows, watching everyday life while it awaits the precise moment to extinguish the life to free the souls.

But… I've had the sad experience to have a conversation with death.

It isn't easy to be face to face with the most feared entity, that which has the power to end, in a second, all the dreams, wishes, and desires that make life.

I'm not going to recount the encounter, per se, but you can read about it in the book *"Signs from the Afterlife"* *[Señales del más allá]*

Death; a shapeless shadow, a dark gauze, cold, moved by an immense love, or a feeling beyond love.

I saw it… With its strange cloak and its empty hood, where only the nothing exists.

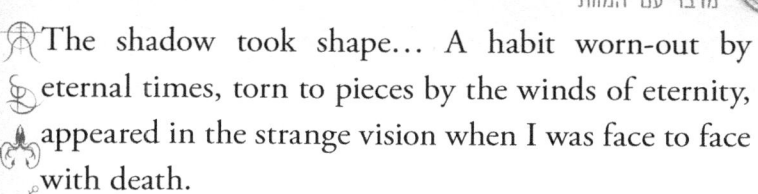

The shadow took shape... A habit worn-out by eternal times, torn to pieces by the winds of eternity, appeared in the strange vision when I was face to face with death.

It began to cover me slowly, my senses were paralyzed, and slowly my spirit was trapped. I appeared in a strange garden, a pasture similar to an infinite wheat field. It was there where the talk with death began.

FACE TO FACE WITH DEATH

Is it my time? I asked with fear, the time has come to abandon life.

No: ...I heard that voice, which isn't of a man or a woman, that voice that has a strange vibration, a sound that touches and resounds in the soul.

מדבר עם המוות

I have just invited you to answer your questions, those that have been left unfinished in our encounter...

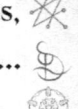

You wanted to know where do the dead go, to discover the mazes that tie the destinies transforming the incarnations.

Today... You will know what is there, beyond death...

You are alive, the world is a hive of routines, you love, you fight, you enjoy life, but... Little is known about death, when I had the chance I venture to seek the macabre answers to the appointment that, someday, everyone would have.

Since the accident, the presence of death and its mysteries aroused in me the curiosity to know the other universe, to know that it exists, not as a legend, but to unravel the secrets of life.

I have to remit the reader to the book **Signs from the Afterlife**, where the near-death experience allowed this encounter, you are entirely free to judge it, at the end it can just be a lie, or someday a reality; maybe after death you will understand.

ויקה

It isn't easy to interrogate death, but I tried to make the regular questions, with some familiarity since the first encounter; the talk was normal and simple.

This is the perfect moment to make public my gratitude to death, not only for this knowledge, but also for so many doors I have known and exposed through the books.

Death is life, and magic is the bridge that joins them... Gratitude...

This is how the dialogue developed... What happens after death?

Well... It said... There is always that same question, once a soul is freed.

Am I dead?

That is the phrase that opens the door to another world, another life, another experience, the transcendental moment when each one will be faced with their conscience.

It is the beginning of a trip with no return, but after death, the ties that are able to fragment the spirit are shown, there are souls that struggle to return, but... These just go thru the corps, they want to hug, but they can't, they want to hold on to their treasures, but they can't even touch them.

Other souls with great loves become too attached, they struggle and suffer to detach from the world, some are unable to do it, sadly, and they remain trapped roaming like ghosts thru time. It isn't easy to leave, when there are many unfinished tasks, material bonds are difficult anchors to cut.

Those who move on to the afterlife, go thru doors with no return to face the judgment of death.

Are you the judge of lives?

No, each one will judge themselves; while wandering thru existence, you safe each one of your actions, all of them, they are printed in your soul, once you are freed from your life memories rush without control, and you... you will be able to see them; you'll be spectator, judge and jury of your life.

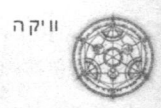

That is the moment, to empty the cup of your soul to fill it once again; it is the instant stopped in time when the guardian of incarnations must be defeated...

In one vision, each one will be judge, jury and the terrible executioner of their actions; it is where the conscience is freed, everything said, everything done, everything that was considered as the most intimate secrets, all life, will be judged.

Unlike existence where you were trapped inside a body, now there are spectators without eyelids, they will watch their existence wander, moment by moment, they won't be able to stop watching everything they have lived.

To be the judge of the life that has just been abandoned in a terrible experience, I am just a silent witness of each judgment, and who is judged won't avoid the evaluation of their actions; by doing so, they could see the options they had, or the damage caused with the consequences generated by their actions.

Is seeing all life without been able to hide or justify; by doing so, the vibration of the spirit will let them know where their soul will flow to. To new incarnations, or to torment. Once you have reached the end of existence, there is nothing keeping the soul tied to the world it has just left.

Life, opportunities, moments, everything has been extinguished; as life is evaluated, it will be deleted forever.

There is no regret, there is no forgiveness, there is no defense in the judgment of death, and I am just a guardian between this instant and eternity.

The path to the new life will depend on the actions taken; either to other incarnations, or to perpetual darkness.

In order to incarnate in another body, in another time, in another space; one must be free from ties to the life one has just left.

If your actions go against life and your opinions, you will, forever, enter in the domains of the nothing; from there, thru the eternity of the worlds, you will never be able to incarnate but, while being locked in the confines of the nothing, throughout eternity, you will wish to live once more, but it will never happen.

Taken actions will be relived, time and time again, you would cry for scape; for another opportunity but... It is freedom, and this is the sentence.

It also happens that, in life, those who commit a crime will live in a prison, according to its severity; either for a period of time, or for their whole life, reliving the crime again and again.

How do you act? How do you know who dies and who doesn't? And, how do you free the soul to stop life?

I've seen so many people die; so much is said about death, but I've never known how you do it.

Is it true that you have a book with the dates in which each one must die?

... The sleeve of the habit floated and, like a thunder, a deep voice said: **Wait, you ask too much; one step at a time...**

TIME TO LIVE

As in a magic act, everything changed, everything around us was now white, I can't find the words to describe the strange event, but everything was white, there was nothing else but the shadow of death and an extreme whiteness, without up or down, nor back or forth... All white... In that moment... A mental blackout, and everything turned dark; it wasn't a color, it was a black mass with conscience, it was there... In the deepest darkness...

It is the nothing... It said...

At the beginning of the material world, the first thing that the great force created was, me, Death; beginning and end, the Alpha and the Omega; or, if you prefer, you can define me as Life.

I am who creates the transformations and mutations of everything that exists. I give life and death, which are life it self.

You must understand that death is an earthly name to identify an end, but I really give life.

Nothing dies to stop existing, everything dies to live. There are infinite physical multiverses and infinite spiritual planes, where the souls can reside.

Everything must change according to its vibration; if you watch carefully, you will notice that nothing really extinguishes; matter continues its perpetual course, recycling itself; an eternal pulse of mutations where, if anything does end, something new germinates.

Death, as such, doesn't exist, but I am who defines the subtle line between one mutation and the other.

Then, no one dies?

Actually. No! Nothing dies; the soul is freed from a particular space-time, in order to live again, in another time, and another space thru another body, or none at all. Or it can incarnate in the no time and no-space, residing in all the multiverses.

What is the soul?

Difficult question to explain and, even more, to comprehend; the soul is everything; more than soul, it is energy. The material universe is formed by different vibrations of energy, some are subtle and others are dense; the subtle is implicit in the dense, as long as it contains it; but, when the vibration of the subtle is stronger than the dense, it is freed.

The powerful and immanent force of the spirit, must flow in the material world; in order to achieve it, it builds bridges; the soul is the energy that allows a spirit to flow through a body, it merges with your body through your soul; it is the sole vibration between both eternities.

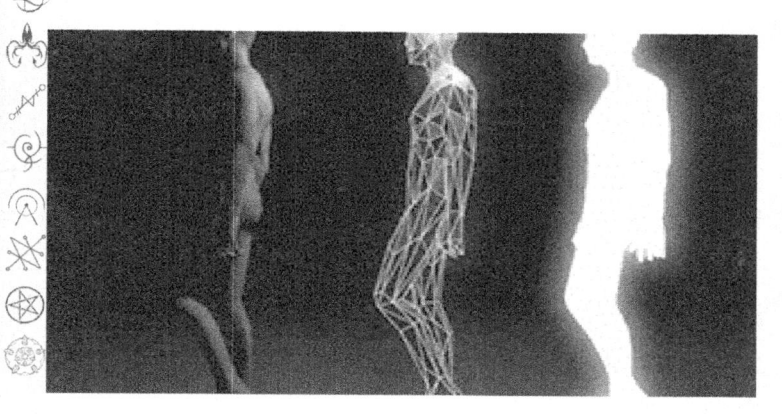

Depending on the scale of the vibration of each soul, the force of a spirit flows in greater or lesser degree.

With each incarnation, the fluidity of the spirit is stronger, until the incarnations stop vibrating in elevated planes of consciousness; worlds that your imagination could never imagine.

CHARLAS CON LA MUERTE

מדבר עם המוות

If you look at a summer night, you'll see millions of stars; they will seem similar, but each one is unique, different, with a conscience of being specific; each one has a different soul and a different vibration.

They fulfill their mission of being; once that mission is fulfilled, they die and transform.

The soul is the energy of knowledge; it is the force of existence; it is the sublime power; the most subtle of vibrations.

All souls have, in them, the power to self discover the wisdom of primary energy; there are young and old souls, but, each time they move forward in a life cycle, the matter can't contain them; that is the moment when I free them; during the judgment, they discover their successes and their mistakes; they incarnate in new life options.

Death doesn't exist.

Those who die are still alive in other dimensions, those who keep the matter, only see the matter; they are living dead who suppose death.

ויקה

You see; cemeteries exist, and what for? The bodies are bodies without souls, but they have the life of transformation that returns them as food for the soil.

They are, have been and continue to be soil, but the human feelings impoverished by selfishness want to maintain the dead as living beings without souls.

A strange way to stop living; and to keep the souls from moving forward.

Each time someone weeps, prays, cries out, begs or curses me, they are ripping the souls that are departing.

No one must weep for the dead; they are souls being freed to new options and lives. The best thing for everyone is to allow the bodies to be dissolved in the fire, the matter returns to the matter, and the soul is free.

Don't talk to tombs or headstones, there is only soil there, the dead are dead.

CHARLAS CON LA MUERTE

How do you choose who must die?

I don't; each one knows when to be free from the body; when the mission is fulfilled, it is time to transmute; I just free the souls, but I don't choose the dates.

Each one decides when to die; since the beginning of life, when your cup is full, it must be emptied; when the cup is empty, it must be filled.

That is the mystery of my sisters, the Moirai, it is the end of your destiny, and it depends on each one to determine when it is time to depart; you will only do it once you mission is fulfilled.

How to know which is the mission?

All destinies are intertwined, if you are in this world, it is because you have a reason more powerful than your conscience, but just because of your actions you will know which one it is; if you do what you are passionate about, that is what you fight for; if you follow your dreams, if you act with all your love for what you wish for; if you push yourself; if you are part of the change of the course of lives; even if

If you don't know your mission, you fulfill it with your actions.

But... If you do what you don't like, if you live in discord; if you have no illusions or dreams; if you live trapped in conformity and submission; if you humble yourself and give up; if you accept resignation as your life; your existence shall be empty for many incarnations.

You must always do something to leave behind after you are gone; that is how the world moves forward, leave something for those who follow, build, teach, show a path for others to travel when you are gone; that is your mission; to do something that leaves a mark when your are gone.

That is how you will stay alive in those who are left behind, and you will vibrate higher, for your new incarnations.

If you are alive, your mission isn't fulfilled; once your mission is over, you will feel that it is time; once this happens "the shadows of death" will appear; they are the signs announcing the departure.

CHARLAS CON LA MUERTE

מדבר עם המוות

Feelings, actions, soul inventories, stripping; you will feel that everything material looses its value; slowly, the releasing of your soul begins, you pick up your steps, the energy radiated throughout your life is collected; these are the sensations and premonitions that everyone can feel when someone is about to leave.

Something inside tells you that a change has arrived, you will tend to live more intensely; you will have more plans, wishes, dreams and desires than ever before; you will want to finish unfinished tasks; you won't know you are going to die but, you will feel the strength of life in all its might.

When the shadows see the releasing of the soul, that is when I appear; that is the sublime moment where the door of the afterlife opens; it isn't something macabre or terrible, although, in order to free the souls, I have to turn to any option; the weapons of death to renew life are varied.

Why some die young, and others don't?

There is no age to die... There is no age to live; if your mission is fulfilled it doesn't matter how long

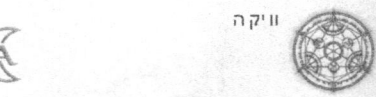

ויקה

your body has been in this world. Your soul will be freed.

Just the presence of a soul in this world changes the destinies of many, even if that presence is just for an instant.

You must know that time is just an earthly factor, just like identity and gender just belong to a body; the soul doesn't have it, and even less, the spirit.

No one dies before it is their time, however, suicide victims choose their time to die; they will travel into eternal darkness.

Others dare to defy death with dangerous actions, without being suicidal, they defy me; if they come to close they will die, even if it isn't their time.

No one can attempt to enter the mazes of death without an invitation, and succeed.

How do you receive that invitation?

The sacred temple of death is entered in spirit, not physically or bodily, you must have the secret keys that open the gates of the old, and to be clear in what you bring in, and what you want to leave with.

Those versed in the arts hold the keys, spells and arcana to come into my domains.

At the beginning of existence, the first to exist were my helpers, who sow the life, they, left the sacred texts about the hidden mazes or underworlds where the power of life is.

But not everyone can enter; it depends on their heart, and their intentions.

Every night your soul leaves your body, and travels into the world of dreams, but... There are other worlds in the dreams; it is your soul who can transmigrate to the world of the dead and return to life; if you learn to control it, you will travel the infraworlds, and will become an accomplice of the shadows.

The power of life is hidden in the world of the dead; the power to transform, change, and make pacts; life for death, death for death, payment for payment; sacrifice or offer.

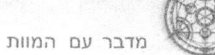

The secret power of life over death, and death over life.

Remember, the earthly concept of death is associated with the end of life, but my presence goes beyond that, it is the death of problems, the death of diseases, difficulties, toughs situations, it is destroying the barriers that restrict, making a pact is to flow in life as long as you live.

That would be eternity?

Nothing dies, everything is everlasting, but if you considerer the temporary space of your incarnation to be real, you will be temporary; the soul and the spirit are what really last; matter is a constant transformation; if you don't free your mind from the matter, you will be trapped in it and consider it as temporary.

And even if it is temporary, the matter is the essence of the eternal energy, thus, it is also eternal, but the stages of matter, or of your body, are temporary. Something that should not matter.

CHARLAS CON LA MUERTE

The concept of life and death divides the capacity to value the moment for incarnation, it holds on to life wishing for the eternity of the body or the matter, instead of taking the maximum advantage of the experience; the matter transmutes, it is born and dies all the time, but, in essence, it is life which changes its form and its end.

Nothing dies, nothing lives forever and still, in essence, it is infinite.

The bodies are shells where the seed emerges, then, they return to the earth to be soil, and then, shells once more. Why would you keep the shell and not the essence?

The physical presence is more valued than the spiritual, turning me into the macabre and unjust Death that ends everything when, in fact, everything begins.

Before they are born, all bodies begin to die, slowly; each second, since birth, begins to age; the body is limited by time; time for a soul to fulfill its mission.

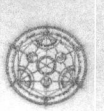

All the events of existence in the short time alive, are experiences that make you fulfill your mission, but, by being in this world, earthly attachments are created, you desire without limits, you want to possess, to have, to be; you accumulate matter as a treasure, you care for it, preserve it, and while doing so, you burry your freedom to be; no one who crosses the boundary between life and death, can bring anything else than their memories, which they will forget; but they don't understand that they can't possess anything, and they can't carry anything.

You live in the attachments; it is considered that life lies in having, in preserving and treasuring, empty lives that end in bitterness and pain when the moment to depart arrives.

Souls that are left trapped without migration, turning into eternal ghosts.

Why do you leave some in limbo, and take others?

I don't leave anyone behind, I can't take nor leave; I only free the souls, each one, according to their vibrations, their actions, their freedom migrates or remains trapped.

CHARLAS CON LA MUERTE

In that freedom, many create bonds so deep with the material world, that when it is their time to die, their soul is freed, but it can't leave, it can't detach and, by doing so, they fragment and tear the spirit, they remain wondering in that mysterious line between life and death.

Eternal ghosts that, just as suicide victims will be free only at the end of time, when I die in the last second.

How can you die if you are death?

I am the first creation of the spirit, I am the bridge between worlds, the spiritual and the material; without me, there is no life; without life, there is no death; in order for a mutation to exist, something has to die to be; multiverses are born, but the change; each change is a death; at the end of time, during the last second, I will be left only with the nothing.

My final day will be a time of deep repose, until the moment a vibration starts a life; and that will be my awakening, to generate life and to take it away, in order to start another cycle. I don't really die; it is just the strange line that connects two eternities.

There is no difference with the normal life of each person; you live one day, one hour, one minute at a time; each second that passes, is a second that, inevitably, dies; each hour, each month, each year, your whole life.

If you know how to extract the real value of each moment, then you will achieve the fullness of life.

- Once you end something, you begin something
- Once a love is born, a love dies
- Once you achieve a goal, the goal losses its value and you reach for another
- All failures are triumphs started at birth
- All fear is hidden courage
- Everyday, you die
- Everyday, you reincarnate
- Every night you travel to the underworld
- Every night is an end, before a new beginning
- Everything is temporary, ephemeral, and transcendental
- Everything is nothing; the nothing is everything
- Nothing dies without being alive; nothing lives without dying, but death, as such, doesn't exist.

CHARLAS CON LA MUERTE

מדבר עם המוות

But you live trapped in ties, in the rush of life, you don't let die to live, you are burdened by the death of your experiences without seeing life hiding and awakening with the new dawn.

You are filled with the past and remain in it avoiding the new dawns, you are buried alive in the memories that torment you the most, dying a little each day, but without living a little each day.

Death exists only in the mind of those who can't see the hidden reality in the secret thalamus of life.

Lives trapped in yesterday's death, ignoring the mutation that exists in each end; nothing ends, everything changes in the next second; nothing is eternal, just the spirit; all else, everything else... Is changeable and mutable.

Your ties, your loves, your supposed possessions, your days, your nights; all of that exists for an instant and then, dies to be born in another extraordinary dawn.

If nothing dies, what happens at the end of life? What happens in that afterlife?

The moment of the release is an extraordinary voyage, no matter how death came to happen, the process is similar; no matter where, when, age, form or place; everything ends in a sole sensation.

It happens in an instant, your mind falls into a deep darkness; everything becomes cloudy, sensations disappear but you are aware; then you are outside of your body, a soft gauze flows entering reality; you exit the illusion of life, all ties to the material world are cut; nothing exists; just you, and me.

You can see your body, but it doesn't matter anymore, you can see the world you just left in a quick vision, like in a momentary dream, and then it disappears, and you are faced with the maximum challenge of life, to defeat me.

You are without being, there is no body, no sensations or emotions, but you will have an infinite and indescribable feeling of peace; there is no physical sensation, you are a free soul.

You can see people who have passed, celestial places; it is the tunnel, the doorway to the afterlife.

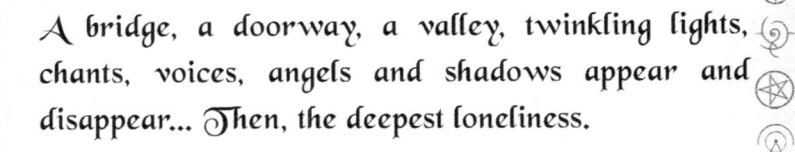

A bridge, a doorway, a valley, twinkling lights, chants, voices, angels and shadows appear and disappear... Then, the deepest loneliness.

Everything vanishes, the sphere of the spirit closes and you are completely alone, it is time to face me.

In that solitude, in the semi darkness, you will feel my presence, not like right now, but when you are free from the material body.

All your senses have disappeared; there will be no fear, nor anxiety, joy or sadness, you know you've died, but you don't care, and you are not sorry for what you've left behind.

Now... now is when you face reality, outside the world of illusions.

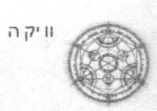

There are no judges or divinities, no judgment or demons that strip your soul?

No, there is no such thing, no one can judge you, no one can sentence you; that is your judgment.

In that solitude... As if you were an observer, you will see your life projected; in that precise instant, in a ghostly vision, you will return to the last moment before your death.

It is chilling to see your corps, but now you see it in a different way; your body, which was home to your soul, doesn't inspire you; you can see how you give it back to me.

Many beings suffer and vibrate when contemplating a body destroyed, unkempt, and withered; how the temple of the soul was raided and destroyed; a corrupt body.

I... deliver the body as portal to the soul, to be cared for, it is your sacred temple as long as you live, I give the freedom to worship and respect it; but, what do you return to death and to the earth? How is your body, the temple to your soul?

In that vision, you understand, you realize that, that body, now inert was the cradle where you learned, felt and lived the life that is now over.

... You begin the process... You contemplate life from afar, your life, your experiences, everything is there; what was done in what is hidden, all your thoughts, all your experiential memory appears reflected...

Slowly you look, judging, remembering, you see your life pass by, your actions, your decisions, your good choices and your failures; everything passes by... And you, evaluate...

It is there when you will have a talk with death.

What did you do with your life?

Seeing your existence, you'll evaluate your experiences; you'll begin with the body you're returning, how do you return it?

Where did you take that body, what life did you give it, how did you use its hands, its feet, its being, which good choices, and mistakes, did you make.

How many mountains did you climb in the challenges you wanted to achieve? Did you make the effort or did you give up?

Were you able to reach your dreams, meet your goals? Did you fight to make your dreams come true?

You are going to assess your life, what you did with it; you've seen it since birth until your death, everything is there now...

I am just going to be your guide, so you can evaluate your existence; from now on, you'll be judge, jury and executioner of your actions.

How to define good and evil; the good choices and mistakes of a life?

There is no good or evil, there is an intention; in the spirit, everything is a different vibration; your judgment will depend on that, once you are dead, each event in your life, no matter how insignificant you think it is, produces a vibration; it then generates a resonance wave that affects all the vibrations in the universe.

Actions motivated by your freedom and your decisions affect every destiny; alter every soul; those that were part of your life, as well as, the new ones that incarnate.

Remember that, even if you are not in the world you left, your actions will remain in it.

You will be alive in what you leave; in the thoughts of those who remember; in those who stay, living their lives.

Every life has a responsibility with the others, close or distant; you will never know and much less understand how destinies are intertwined; how one action affect the future, one seed sown, although the sower doesn't exist, it will germinate in all possible futures.

Understanding each person's mission, assessing good and evil, is something that transcends beyond the universes of time, life and death.

In the profound nature of the essence of the spirit, there is neither one nor the other; actions are events that last, modifying the futures in one way or another.

The concept that one has of justice while you are incarnated differs from the value with that of the spirit.

What is evil?

To destroy, kill, brake, alter, cause pain, generate suffering, take advantage of the weak, any synonym of destruction; that is the concept in life.

But, what do you know about the reasons of the spirit; it is here, during the assessment, that all actions have future consequences, both in your incarnations as in the life you leave behind.

No one knows the mission they have, and its consequence; in life, bad can be good, and vice versa.

An assassin, a rapist, a predator, the most violent and dangerous being, is an instrument of wisdom; but, be careful with the judgments, remember that each one has in their hands the power to choose and decide; the freedom.

Those who vibrate in the destruction will have destruction in their incarnations.

Keep in mind that the most important thing is the intention that moves the actions.

The only way to fight evil is with a greater evil; one has to be worst, but it isn't moved by evil, but by good.

Even that good, ends up being evil; you can only know what it is by looking at the causes generated by the actions in the chain of possible futures.

Someone who is born very ill, with great suffering, and difficulties is, apparently, cause of sadness and pain.

But you only see the pain; if you look, the presence of that being, in those conditions, changes destinies and futures; the doctor, the science, the advance in treatments; that suffering being becomes the "salvation" of many.

The soulless killer, with his cruel and destructive actions, brings changes to the future; safety, prevention, controls, every negative event is the cause that teaches and generates great transformations. Each one in their judgment evaluates, not only the action caused, but also the causes generated.

Collectively, souls learn from suffering and adversity, destructive events are the school that teaches to avoid them.

So, they will always take place, not as the destruction, but as an inevitable part of knowledge.

How to judge evil from good, or good from evil if you ignore its effect in the future?

What is good?

To be happy, to win, achieve realizations; there is no way to define what is good; to make others happy, to live fully, to find harmony and stability.

To be good is the opposite of being evil but... How to define the mysterious line between one and the other?

When you see your life, you evaluate your actions and their consequences; maybe driven by a deep feeling of love, you give, you deliver, you try to be good, to be the best but, only bring bad in the future, for making incapable those who live from you; and, what will be of them once you die?

- To give isn't to help
- To be servile isn't kindness
- To work and to live for and by other, is undeserving
- To be good, is to end up causing evil

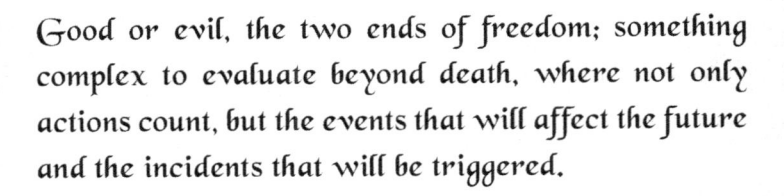

Good or evil, the two ends of freedom; something complex to evaluate beyond death, where not only actions count, but the events that will affect the future and the incidents that will be triggered.

The freedom you are born with gives you options to act, each act is a vibration wave that your soul receives and stores; at the end of your life, when you die, you will see which vibrations you have.

According to these, you will start a new incarnation.

No one can make judgment about the actions, except for one self, not only they are the acts or the intention in freedom; it is the sum of passed causes, lost opportunities, cultures, creeds, religions, dogmas, family influences; different events modify the essences and the spirits, the struggle for survival unleashes unknown forces and wild or heroic actions; no one can judge these actions, only each one, from within, evaluates the options they had.

Every action is linked to the incidents that provoked it, and the events it will provoke; something bad can end up being good, and the good can be even worst than the bad.

While in your judgment, you are not only evaluating your life, but everything you have done; how, in your freedom, did you create your destiny, and the destiny of others.

Then, there is no good or evil, nor justice, or punishment, neither heaven or hell; those who act wrong, damage, destroy, provoke suffering; there is no punishment after death, and at the same time, who leads a righteous life, seeking well-being, doesn't have a prize. Is there not a heaven so desired or a hell so feared?

No, the spirit doesn't take sides, it is your freedom; punishment or prize are earthly concepts, just like male or female gender, love or hate, wealth or poverty, identity; those are concepts of life.

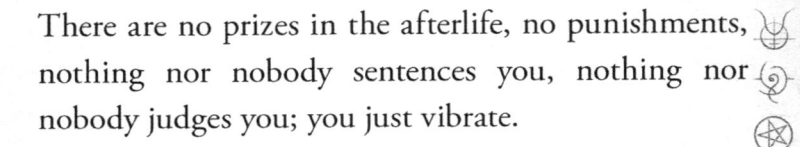

There are no prizes in the afterlife, no punishments, nothing nor nobody sentences you, nothing nor nobody judges you; you just vibrate.

And the vibration of a life either lifts you or annuls you; depending on your decisions, you attract and vibrate in the different scales; after death, souls can't suffer or be happy.

Happiness or suffering, it is a mental state while you inhabit a body, they are the emotions that touch the soul, but, they don't exist in a soul without a body.

Prize or punishment is a judgment concept while you are alive; it doesn't last after death; even though the living long for, or suppose of, the actions of a divine justice.

Where the bad goes to suffer, and the good is showered with benefits; ones to hell, and others to heaven.

That doesn't exist, but, the vibrations of the life left behind, push you to certain incarnations, not to expiate your guilt, they don't exist, but until you vibrate in the balance.

PUNISHMENT

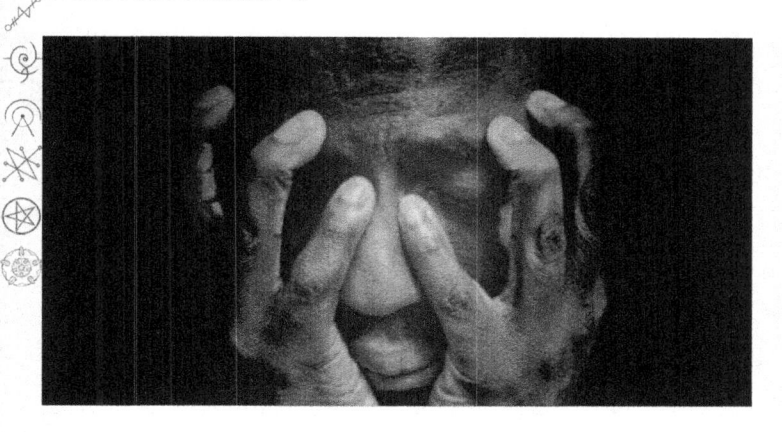

When vibrating in each act of your life, you generate a frequency, your soul is filled with experiences based on you decisions; these, generate the bases of your new incarnation.

While in your judgment, you assess; it is there where you could think that hell exists.

When assessing your life, the events that generated alterations stand out; those that, under your freedom, transformed destinies, causing pain, suffering and agony.

CHARLAS CON LA MUERTE

מדבר עם המוות

It is when your acts and your decisions bring you to a state of spiritual freezing; you relive, time and time again, the acts that brought suffering.

You are trapped in your visions, reliving the events, time and time again; you see the consequences of your actions, all the destinies you altered, all the souls you brought suffering to; you will see each event, time and time again, for eternity.

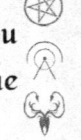

And, if in your freedom, your life was to destroy the lives of others, you won't have how to avoid your sentence, but remember; in the spiritual world it isn't just the occurred act, but also the consequences it brought. So, think well how you act.

Time doesn't exist in this maze, time and time again, you will see the sequence, and the consequence you left; you can't change it or repeat it, feel what others felt, assess your decisions, time and time again.

This delays your future incarnations; after reliving and understanding that every action has a consequence, you enter to a dark universe, and then... Once your soul is free from those vibrations, you incarnate again; you have the option of a new

ויקה

life; that is if you manage to come back; otherwise, your soul will remain trapped in your actions, for perpetuity.

Living and reliving exactly the same, feeling the pain you caused, time and time again; that who is the cause of a life of pain, will live in pain; that is the vibration chosen.

If you say that everything is forgotten during the judgment; why is such purgatory produced?

For a soul to incarnate it must be in a specific vibration, harmonized; that way, the knowledge acquired from previous incarnations flows in the life that begins.

Nature doesn't self destroy, if it were so, it wouldn't exist; it doesn't allow for destruction to go from one incarnation to the other.

If you see life as it is, you can appreciate that the souls incarnate with deeper knowledge, humanity moves forward for the benefit and greatness, the conquest, and the better life.

But, in occasions, education, culture, creed and others, push souls to make the wrong decisions of destruction, convinced they are doing good.

By doing so, their vibrations change; the act produces that alteration, and it must be harmonized before an incarnation.

All souls are intertwined; those who are alive, share the same time, the same space, they are connected in one-way or another; they are supports for everyone to fulfill their missions.

In each life, you have the freedom to choose and act, they are your decisions, while you harmonize your life, you will be completely aware; it is where many phenomena are produced, where those who are left, feel the presence of those dead.

It is similar to what happens in nature, if a hyena attacks the others, these, either chase it away or they kill it.

If a young is born different, mother or father will destroy it, so it won't interfere with the others.

In nature, the representation of the spirit is similar, actions generate changes, but it differs in the judgments.

Just as in life, when a person commits a crime, is retired from society unable to live in it; the person is sentenced as a prisoner, locked up in a jail sail; the punishment can be as long as their life; many live a life of confinement for their actions.

Unlike the laws of life, in the afterlife, the judgment isn't only about the act caused, but also about the consequences that precede them.

If someone is unfaithful; in life one just sees the infidelity and it is condemned, but fails to understand what is inside of the soul. What happened before to get to the point of infidelity? And, What will happen to being unfaithful? Maybe, it will be happiness, even if the other person is unhappy, how will they be judged?

A scammer, with the heart of an entrepreneur, moved by necessity turns to cheating; knows the strategies, discovers the art, they are judged and sentenced to many years in jail, but another soul, with wisdom,

CHARLAS CON LA MUERTE

מדבר עם המוות

turns them into the master that will teach how to avoid future scams. Which would be the verdict. Guilty or innocent?

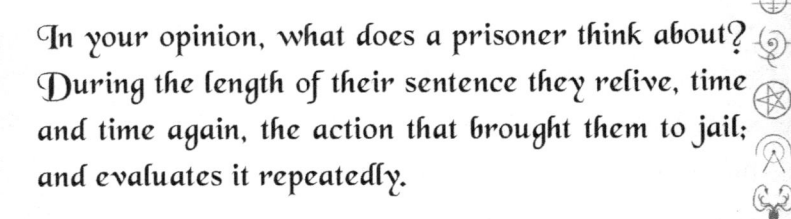

In your opinion, what does a prisoner think about? During the length of their sentence they relive, time and time again, the action that brought them to jail; and evaluates it repeatedly.

It is purified and harmonized, in the afterlife, you will live something similar, but each one imposes their sentences; there is no time, but there are incarnations.

What you have learned during your life, in the fight between good and evil, that is the judgment of an action; but you never evaluate the rest, an infinite of events that agreed for that to happen, and the infinite causes that said action will produce.

Each one will be their defendant during the judgment of death.

Everything that has been said to you, god and demon, judgments, sentences, infernal suffering, heavenly blessings; these are human judgments of soul actions; those that are left in the earthly world.

וויקה

Occasionally, the limits of wisdom are incomprehensible to incarnated souls.

Be ware of the judge or the jury, while in the journey of life; many sentence what they hold in their hearts; sometimes, the condemning judge is guiltier than the person being condemned.

Each action provides infinite knowledge in all souls; that is what defines guilty or innocent.

The judgment of death, the judgment of each, where you move forward, or are held back, once freed from the body.

This is why you should think, calmly, about your actions; while you are incarnated, your conscience blurs the life after death; you live in everyday life, but you ignore the actual value of "being alive", and even more, you ignore the deep effects of the judgment of death, those that will affect the incarnations.

Maybe you think it doesn't exist, but the shadows of those trapped, scream during the nights the pain of having to relive their suffering for eternity, without being able to end their torture, to see, time and time again the event that torments them.

And what about forgiveness, remorse? It is said that everything is forgiven in the afterlife, something like forgetting sins and the purification of the soul; it is said that souls must die in peace in order to transcend.

What is forgiveness?

Incarnated souls use it as a shield to please and magnify the souls of those who forgive, not of whom is forgiven.

The act done, is done; so forgiveness can't undo it; when someone forgives, they are exalted as long as the forgiven is in their debt; a debt that will never pay.

If you pay attention, you will understand that many say, "forgive", but no one can judge and much less, condemn. In life, as well as in death, it depends on the intention; for some, a sin is a fatal error, or a mistake; but you only learn from errors and mistakes.

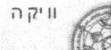

And, if learning is a sin, there will be no incarnation of the souls, and much less the freedom.

Once again, the wisdom with which each soul is provided before incarnating is freed during life while facing life; the most difficult moments allow that force to flow; causes and destinies free the interior knowledge of other lives.

That is how human progress grows in all the areas of life; there is no sin, or the error that is a mistake or a sin. The architect learns more about the houses that are destroyed, than from those that are still standing.

All failures are the sum of knowledge for the coveted success. How is that knowledge a sin?

Not even during the judgment of death there is forgiveness; because there is no sin.

But during life, many take advantage of that to pretend to forgive; those who say to forgive assume for their vibration the sins of others; they become sin eaters, no one has authority over the freedom of souls, besides me.

Tell me your sins that I will absolve you; that sentence doesn't belong to any incarnated soul, it can't forgive; but it assumes, for itself, the supposed sins; only that who says to forgive sins is who accepts the sin, thus, they feed from sins, and in their freedom, they will answer for the acts.

COMPREHEND

In their freedom, each soul has the wisdom to comprehend, to know that other souls, in the release of their interior knowledge, motivated by the essence of the spirit, act through life, discovering their power. In that act you learn, and you only learn by failing. Understanding failure, you encourage knowledge and the learning that will transcend in the incarnations.

But dogmatic influences and believes blind the reason; they take you to deep pain and suffering abyss, by imposing on sins and forgiveness. You did something that others consider to be a sin or inappropriate.

Before that, ask yourself:

- What did you learn from that act?
- What experience and knowledge did it leave?

- What caused it, and what consequences followed?
- Would you do it again?

Those questions, and more, can only be answered in time, not before; the seed of the act has been sowed, and you must wait for the fruit; that way, you will know the answer.

Thus, since there is no sin, there is no forgiveness; much less, there is no payment to be forgiven.

Sin has been imposed as a limitation tool, don't think, don't feel, don't act, don't do, don't wish; avoid temptation and don't try; almost all your actions are considered sins, and, by accepting it, you stop living; you are mentally submitted, you relinquish your life; what ever you do, it will never be a sin, it is your experience, the sum of your experiences;

CHARLAS CON LA MUERTE

מדבר עם המוות

a doubt, it gives you knowledge, and the sum of knowledge, will make you wise.

REMORSE

There is no way to undo what has been done, remorse is a senseless false promise, a refuge from the storm, a manipulation done with the intention to improve.

A farce created to hide decisions and desires; remorse is just words.

But, if you consider you have committed an act that caused pain, take two actions that produce happiness; that is make up for your actions; when you die, and are facing the judgment of death, you will watch those decisions.

Before you try to compensate for your actions, always avoid taking them. Why do it? If you know, before hand, that it is something destructive.

Always think before you act, deep inside your essence lies the eternal wisdom that allows you to run your destiny.

If you are certain, do it; nothing is stopping you; take the challenge to try, and if you fail, don't regret it; assume your experience as knowledge, but always reach for balance; if you damaged something, fix it.

You can't win without giving something in return, that is the perpetual and natural law, in life as well as in death.

Don't stop to follow your dreams, fight to find them, don't make excuses if you don't reach them; maybe you need to renounce to many things in your life that are a burden; it is you, and that is the only thing your bring with you when you die.

Never regret! Remove that from your mind. Remember; you learned something.

PENANCE

You don't have to submit your soul to penances that destroy you more than redeemed you; what is done is done; and what ever you do, you won't undo. What is the reason to blame yourself, condemn yourself, and punish yourself? Maybe, in the future, you will realize that your act served a purpose.

CHARLAS CON LA MUERTE

מדבר עם המוות

It is useless to torture the flesh, when your act comes from your soul; what is the use to pay a man money, if the action is yours; you can't cleanse your soul with lashes or prayers, even less by giving charity, nor cleaning you conscience with the false believe of a redeemer that intercedes for your alleged sins.

There is no greater indignity or mistake, than a soul flagellating and destroying the body it occupies; they impose the false believes to destroy your flesh and your soul. When you die, you will realize, even more, about the deceit and how you wasted your life.

But, if you consider you did harm, also act in order to fix it, healing the wound you caused.

If you do harm, you will never fix the damage caused by repenting, condemning, paying for forgiveness and doing penance. It is your act, already done.

What you want to do is to find that someone you have hurt and fix the damage with acts and gestures that reestablish the balance, not with a whip over your back; if you do that, it will be useless for the other person.

ויקה

But incarnated souls cause pain and sorrow, later they confess and blame themselves, they are absolved and forgiven for a few coins; the sin eater assumes the sin, but the victim is never repaired.

What is the use of everything done, if the damage is still caused?

Maybe you will find refuge in a false believe, and consider that you are safe, but... here you will see the reality; your reality.

There is no worst hell than an altered conscience, filled with pain and suffering; those who cause pain and deceit, dwell with pain and deceit in their souls.

There is no greater heaven than a clean conscience; those who clean it and act wisely dwell with harmony in their souls.

No one, not even I, can touch your soul; only you can alter it, calm it; you can tarnish it or upraise it.

Then, are the shadows souls that grieve? Why do they remain in the world of the living, if they are dead?

CHARLAS CON LA MUERTE

מדבר עם המוות

Your actions in life perpetuate you after death.

Some have caused so much pain and suffering, either by imposing it or by receiving it, that their souls don't migrate. They remain trapped between two worlds; they are aware they are dead, but they consider themselves to be alive; it is eternal suffering.

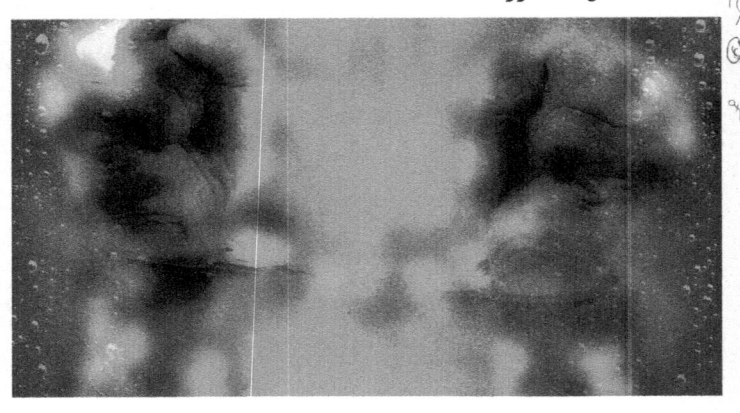

SOULS WITHOUT BODY

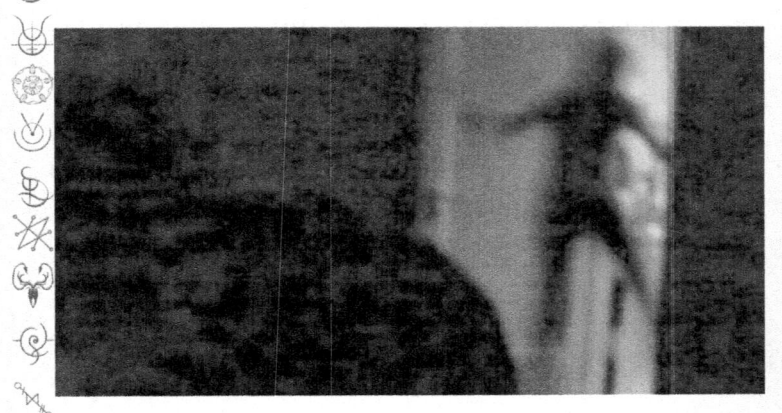

Bonds created throughout existence, difficult to break, bonds that fragment the spirit, and corrupt desires, keep them tied to a world that no longer exists for them.

Some of the shadows, of suicide victims as well as of those that remain to be freed, will remain trapped for eternity until the death of death.

The fragile line between life and death is an impassible abyss; the shadows are the living reflection that after death, there is life; other incarnations, but it will all depend on the actions, just on the decisions made; to move forward, or to stay.

Is there a way to help those who didn't move on, so they are able to do it and avoid them the suffering? Maybe prayers, rituals or masses; how can you avoid being trapped?

The dead are dead; shadows are shadows; no one can do anything for them; only they can free themselves from their ties.

If someone dies tied to their treasures, they can't posses them; but, they see in anguish how others enjoy them; as long as they don't understand they no longer have any belongings, they will continue to be tied to a treasure that no longer exists. But they can't accept it.

Who could explain it to them?

After destroying their body, the soul of the suicide victim continues to be trapped; only I have the power to give life and death.

But, by making their decision, their soul doesn't migrate to new incarnations; free from the body, it makes a judgment on themselves, they see their whole life, but see the life that was left to live; free from the conscience, they will only observe the best of what they could have had; the best decisions, even the moment when they should have died.

When they get to that moment, they go back to see their suicide, the complete sequence; and in that second time, they can observe the consequences of their actions, what they left in the world they abandoned; and they will continue like this for the eternity of times; living without living.

In their freedom, their decision; there is no way to help them.

THE BONDS

Since birth, you form bonds with the material world and with the souls with whom you share and incarnation.

Bonds are strengthened by time; slowly you discover the power of possessing; you loose the spiritual sense for the material sense.

You hoard, possess, have; arrogance makes its appearance; you give value to the material, and forget the spirit.

Occurs with everything, money, wealth, love, and work; you accumulate too much.

Unfortunately, you begin to hold on to your possessions, they are your life, you brag about having, you loose the real sense of life and, if you don't know how to act, you will end up being a slave of the possessions; those that will trap your soul.

But, if you have dreams and have been able to achieve them, always remember, what legacy you leave to the world after you die?

It isn't to leave wealth for those who have never conquer it; it is to leave paths for other to walk on to climb their mountains.

But you can only do that while you are alive; once you are dead, you won't have a choice; it doesn't matter if you leave a will with your requests; it must be you, in life.

You are a body created from the soil, your soul isn't from the soil, just as your mind; your soul is nestled and freed from your body.

The soil from your body vibrates with the material world, and your soul inside of it; but nothing material can touch your soul; nor your soul can act over matter, which is done thru your body.

When you die, your soul is freed; you can't take anything material, but possessions can trap your soul.

The more bonds you make with the material world, once you die, they will be very hard to brake; they will fragment your spirit, tearing your soul. You will remain in the material world, without being able to stop it.

Love and sexual desire comes from the body, not the soul; feelings are emotions, bonds generated when you wish to have love and bodies; when you die, those bonds will destroy your soul, if you didn't know how to act.

CHARLAS CON LA MUERTE

מדבר עם המוות

Do all ghosts remain trapped? Or, some find the path to incarnate?

There are deaths not caused by me; a murder, in its freedom, takes the life of another; deaths that should not occur; dreams and illusions are cut short.

Others, in their freedom, abuse, rape, destroy and murder; they cause great pain and suffering.

Some of the souls that are freed in a violent way remain temporarily trapped while destinies are moved; these are souls that disrupt other souls to complete something in their mission.

Some become the torment of the souls that brought them harm, until they see them destroyed.

Justice or vengeance is the right of every soul, which acts after a sudden death; it is the sentence of the soul that destroyed it when its mission was not even finished.

ויקה

מדבר עם המוות

The world of shadows is a world of indescribable terror; freed souls that torment incarnated souls; no one can help. It is a bridge that only involves the soul of the victim and its executioner; no one has power over this.

As long as the executioner is alive, he is the only one that can free the soul that he destroyed; the acts, just the acts...

- Life for life
- Death for death
- Payment for payment
- Sacrifice or offering

The cycle is the same, the compensation is spiritual, and freedom is the condition. It depends on each one.

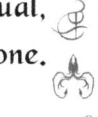

When these precepts are met, destroyed souls begin the journey to new incarnations.

ויקה

PRAYERS TO THE DEAD

מדבר עם המוות

Anything you do for those who lay dead works for the path of the incarnations; it may work for those who are still alive, but not for those who have departed.

Prayers, gifts, masses, petitions, novenaries, pleas, requests; anything you can think of, and do, for those who die, doesn't work.

The dead are dead; there are no bonds with life and where they are going; it is a solitary journey; it is where each one is faced to the judgment of death.

Those who are left try, in vane, to compensate for wrongful acts committed with the one who died; prayers and pleas that only ease a guilty conscience.

ויקה

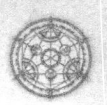

These prayers are for the living, they do nothing for the dead; nor exorcisms to free trapped souls; none of that can be done; they are of my domain, and no living being can defy the freedom of the souls, and much less, death.

On the contrary, the best thing you can do for those who die is to FORGET THEM; they are dirt without soul that must return to the earth, that is why it is important to know, in life, What are you going to leave in this world when you die?

It isn't about wealth or material things, those are from this world. What footprint will your soul leave in its path thru the earth?

Nothing can be done for the dead, you can only do for the living; masses and celebrations of death, that is only to attract the shadows of death; leave the dead in peace; don't visit cemeteries, don't keep remains of the dead, don't invoke those who have departed during mass; and never ask for actions from the afterlife; you are alive, they are dead; they can't hear you.

CHARLAS CON LA MUERTE

מדבר עם המוות

But, if you do, the shadows will appear; you must not interact with them unless you know how to control them.

Although there are doors to enter to my domains, in life; you must know very well the keys to open them, and not end up with a live body with a soul trapped in death.

Then, is there a way to communicate with the dead? To be able to invoke those who have died? There are stories that tell that a medium can do it.

Isn't up to the living, but to the dead; some souls, that are still wondering, can contact the living; once the soul has migrated, every connection with the life it just abandoned is lost.

But be careful with my allies, the shadows, they can impersonate any spirit; don't attempt to enter the domain of the dead if you don't know how to exit.

Always be careful with my allies, if you invoke them, don't doubt that they will come; you must know the keys that open and close the door to the world of the dead; and be even more careful with the souls that

ויקה

wonder, you will attract them, but they won't leave when you want them to; you will turn your life into a life of horror.

To dream about the dead, does it mean they are communicating?

Dreams are temporary deaths, and in them, you run into those who are dead, but it isn't their spirits; you communicate with their footprints left.

In dreams you discover another life, memories or echoes of time that each soul leaves in their path thru the world.

They appear as guides, beings of light, souls of harmony, demons of vengeance, beings of mundane pleasures, infernal or celestial visions; every dream about the dead is a message of life.

If you want, you can make sacred pacts with me of with the shadows to avoid that those echoes or footprints left by the dead act destroying your life.

Some; experts in the secrets of the afterlife are able to control the shadows and the spirits of the world

CHARLAS CON LA MUERTE

מדבר עם המוות

of dreams; just as many entities manifest as familiar dead to control and feed from your soul. *(Refer to the book: Duat The Sacred Book of the Dead [Duat El libro Sagrado de los Muertos])*

Between the fragile line that separates life and death, there is an infinite of underworlds where shadows dwell.

Some people annul their soul by leaving their body at the mercy of the shadows; these are the mediums, the real ones; they transmit knowledge and wisdom; they allow themselves to connect with the prints left by the souls of light; that print is perpetual, it expresses its light and wisdom thru the temporary body.

But there is the risk of a dark entity appearing as a being of light, and someone close to the medium, or even them, could die under terrible torment.

Instead of making attempts to act with the dead, it is best to spend your time acting with the living.

Only those who know the paths can enter in my domains; the rest must avoid it.

ויקה

Remember, at the beginning, my shadows and I gave life, they, left their most deepest secrets about life and death; secrets that have been forgotten with time; today, life is considered to be the constant, even though you live with death, you have lost the real value of life.

Few understand that the judgment of death is the transmigration of the souls to new incarnations; it must be understood that nothing is eternal.

If you are death, why do others produce it? Isn't it your hand that moves the hand of the killer?

Each person acts in their freedom, and, it is in that freedom that exist those who usurp the work of death; I don't move the hands of the killers, nor their souls;

I have infinite ways to free them without the need to turn to other souls.

My shadows know the secrets and the ways to do it. When someone must disincarnate, the shadows know it before hand; slowly the abandonment begins, and, in the end, it is me who takes the soul.

Killers are moved by other interests, that who takes a life, pays with a life; the sequence is long, sons, parents, friends, family, etc. Wars, destruction and chaos.

If a lion kills another lion, the fittest domains; but its domain is temporary, someday, another lion will take its life.

No one lives longer than they are supposed to in the cycle of life and death, but...

The killer makes the decision to kill, no matter the weapon or the form; the intention is to destroy one or many lives.

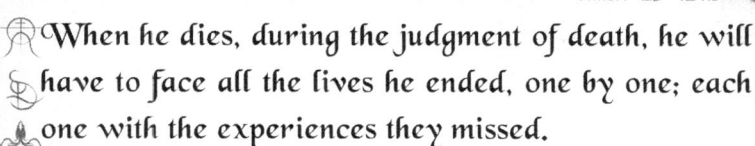

When he dies, during the judgment of death, he will have to face all the lives he ended, one by one; each one with the experiences they missed.

But, as said before, during the judgment he will see what happened before, and what will happen after his actions.

What pushed him to commit it, what options he had, how could he avoid it, or was he innocent; once it is over, he will vibrate according to his evaluation. Many souls of killers are frozen for eternity; he who causes a death due to poor decisions assumes death.

A killer who takes a life, his judgment will depend on the act; the killer who kills a murdered, what moves him?

To fight evil, you always need a greater evil; it depends on the intention.

The most relevant thing about existence, lies between life and death, life; as the option to develop, reach, move forward, discover knowledge, achieve goals and dreams, find the sense for being alive, everything that this means.

Life is the marvelous opportunity to have a true conscience, which allows you to discover the limits of the spirit.

Death is the abrupt cessation of all the possibilities, no one is safe from death, but it happens once the mission is finished; but that who decides to kill, for whatever the reason, assumes the burden of that life, for himself.

However, it always depends on the intention; what ever existed before, and the consequences after.

Now, to kill, is a complex act to define, it covers all the living, animals, plants, insects, humans, and inhuman; there are probable reasons to commit these acts, a life is a life; it is the game of vibrations and decisions.

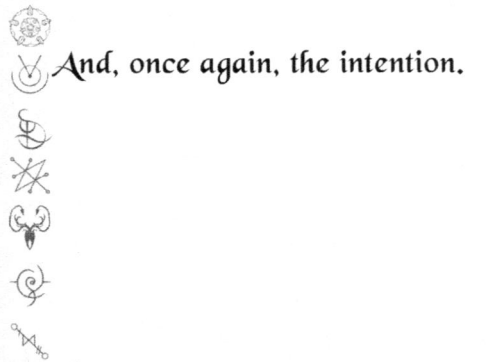

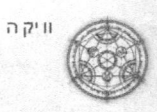

And, once again, the intention.

REASON AND INSTINCT

You must understand that, in the judgment of death, you must separate carnal from divine; the soul is incarnated in an animal body, it possesses survival instincts, spontaneous actions that don't answer to desire or intention.

What would you do if an animal attacks your child?

What would you do if someone attacks him?

You react; sometimes you reason and try to evaluate, but others, you could take the life of the attacker to safe your child.

The options are infinite, thus, it is for the judgment of death to evaluate the actions. In it, you will have to assume the consequences.

I can understand that, it is similar to life; but what happens to the disasters where so many people die? Did they complete their mission simultaneously? Or, in your freedom, since you are death, do you take lives without a reason?

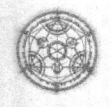

In the universe, nothing has been so harshly judged than me. I have been sentenced and cursed, feared; false and strange concepts are created, but the reality is different.

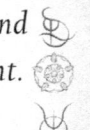

I can't interfere when disasters happen, I am not happy, nor I like, loosing the lives of so many who have dreams and desires to live; of those who haven't completed their missions, but must depart for other reasons. They die also, but the causes are not my wish.

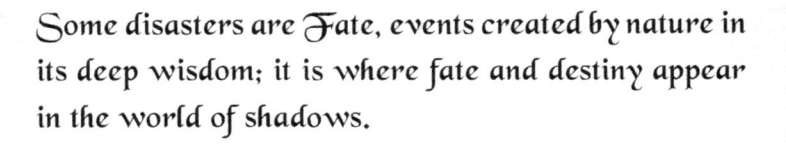

Some disasters are Fate, events created by nature in its deep wisdom; it is where fate and destiny appear in the world of shadows.

In a catastrophe, some are saved, others die; it is fate who decides; those who have made pacts with me have protection, and save their lives to continue.

Other disasters are created by the decisions made by someone else; an airplane pilot with emotional problems drags many destinies to their end.

A negligent mechanic makes the decision to do his work poorly; an architect uses the wrong materials; and the list goes on; those decisions end in disaster. It isn't my doing.

These are decisions made by men that cut short the destinies of men.

What happens to those who die without completing their mission?

They return to the same time, and the same space; they incarnate bodies close to where they lived, family who has unexpected children; children with similar looks and tastes to someone who died in a disaster; children who remind us of events or specific situations, but should not have to know it.

In fact, many people feel that they have lived in certain places or situations; they feel strong attractions, they are related, share tastes; these are souls that meet in other lives.

When asked about a topic, each one discovers that they know more than they suppose, but ignore why; how many times do you ask yourself if you have lived what you are living; or you keep memory flashes of other lives, but you never find an answer to why you fear me. Maybe, these are memories of your deaths.

CHARLAS CON LA MUERTE

מדבר עם המוות

... The phenomenon of déjà vu, has demonstrated that type of apparent coincidences; stories where experiences from another life are perceived, but can't be defined; strong attractions to someone you don't know, but is extremely familiar.

Are those souls that meet again thru incarnations just the result of disasters or lives cut short?

No, they are souls whose bonds in life have been so strong that they follow each other thru incarnations, but remember there is no sexual gender, so it is different in each incarnation, but the attraction is more powerful than destiny.

Those who incarnate to complete a mission, die once it is finished; these are deaths that few understand, healthy children, young people with a life, who only live for a while, complete their mission and leave.

And God?

Which god?

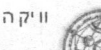

ויקה

מדבר עם המוות

ויקה

CHARLAS CON LA MUERTE

מדבר עם המוות

I am the end, in every creed, religion, dogma, concept and believe, I am Death, attacked, condemned, cursed, macabre, and all the derogative synonyms they can add.

I am fought, just like it happens with the devil; I am the shadow of misfortune, the representation of tragedy, the worst of omens, in one way or another, you struggle to fight me, annul me, destroy me; you scream and profess that death must be defeated.

How far and different reality is, I am not an adversary to no one, I don't generate wars nor seek victories; I don't destroy, nor I end dreams. I am just the life that has to mutate, I am who opens the doors to incarnations; I am who hands the thread of the destinies for the Moirai to weave.

The concepts and ignorance about death lead to strange proclamations, they blame me, in masses, rituals, ceremonies, exorcisms; keep death as far away as possible; the most feared thing in life; without realizing that I am not the enemy, on the contrary, I am an ally to those who really live.

The sellers of gods claim to have power over death, they create stories, exploit, use and manipulate, they sell the terror of my presence, and they sell the salvation of the soul. But they don't sell that the salvation of the souls doesn't depend on me, but on each one.

There is no god that can defeat me, it doesn't exist, and no one can scape me. I am the beginning and the end, I give live and I take it.

But God... Is just an earthly concept, where to hide human fears, god, is the refuge of the weak, mediocre who don't value the power they posses, and need an imaginary entity to live.

God is the reason to act or not; god is the wrong believe that limits the spirits that loose the opportunity to be incarnated, discovering the power they posses.

There are so many gods created that they have become the death of incarnated souls.

There is nothing or nobody, that limits your path, you are free to reach your dreams, discover your horizons, learn and make mistakes; discover in your errors the deep knowledge you acquire when failing your desires, the immeasurable value of experience.

There is no sin without forgiveness; there is no redemption without existence; nothing keeps you from being what you desire, but... Act wisely.

No god, anywhere, has defeated death.

And Jesus? He is supposed to be resurrected

Do you know what you say? Or do you consider that, it is true because it is in a book? Don't you see that the judgment of the dead is of each one, and not of a god; the earthly world is filled with gods, but there is only one death, Me.

They sell you a redeemer, who is resurrected among the dead, as they say; there is no one, in the universe, who has entered in the domain of death, gone through its limits, and came back to life.

But there are thousands, millions, that have been dead and incarnate again; they enter to the point of no return, they reach the end, but it is still not the time for them to die; they come back to life but, they value more their existence after they have seen the paths of death.

They have told you so many things after death; a god will judge you; those who sell a god, have turned me into a business of buying and selling souls; heavens are offered for tithe; you are freed from judgment and don't go to hell.

You are threatened that a god will be your judge; that he keeps a book with all you acts; that you have to be mean, conformist, nothing, in order to save you for eternal life.

You don't realize that there can't exist eternal life; there is the eternity of the spirit, but nothing and no one earthly is eternal.

Flesh is earth and earth is, all your desires, feelings, emotions, pleasures; everything you can get to feel is carnal; when you die, your flesh will be just a corps without feelings, and your soul will be free from them.

So, you won't be able to enjoy heavenly pleasures, nor you will have the suffering of the eternal fire.

Everything that happens to your soul in the afterlife will be within you, in your experiences, in your actions; if you are sentenced in your judgment, your soul retires living in those acts for eternity.

Where do souls come from? How do they enter the body and how do they disincarnate?

When the nothing took form creating the material world, it dissolved itself in its insides, during that deep meditation.

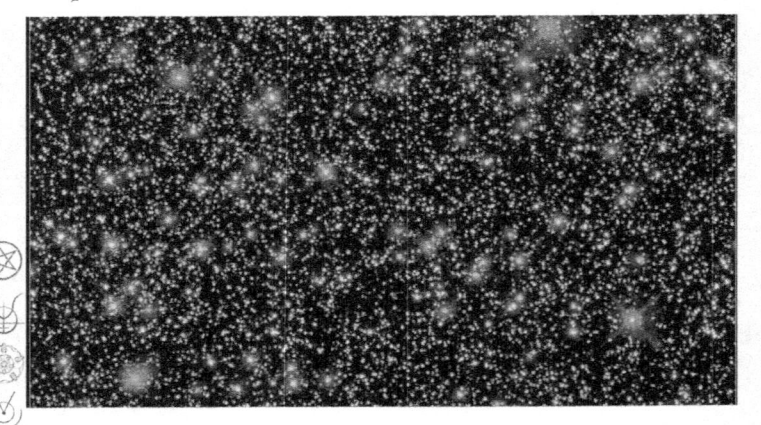

All possible material universes, everything that can exist in shapes, places, times and spaces, they are alive in the meditation of the nothing or the spirit. There is no existence that escapes from the nothing; that primal nothing slowly dissolves into subtle energies, spirits of everything it has created, dense energies that are the matter, as you know it.

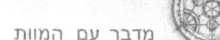

As matter is temporary, and the spirit is eternal; it dissolved in an infinity of spirits, each one with a complete individuality and freedom; a part of that Everything fused with Everything.

Because it is such a subtle energy, it must incarnate temporarily in the material world; it advances in different incarnations as it releases its deep knowledge.

Every instant of an instant of the eternities, millions of new spirits are freed from the Gulf of nothing to incarnate in a material body; the spirit fuses with the soul, and then it incarnates.

Each one has the complete knowledge, but it is concentrated, like in a seed; it is released thru the different incarnations.

While facing life with all its options and alternatives when you are alive, you release this knowledge; you will never learn something you already know.

Why do you think you like something, or you are attracted by it? You have many gifts, you are born with them, that knowledge flows thru your incarnations.

If you look at human history, there are other souls in other bodies and places, but in the recent human history, you will easily understand how that knowledge is developed in favor of life. Each soul that incarnates brings with it the experience of its previous life.

When the end of time arrives, the nothing will be Everything; it will be perfect.

It will have all the possible knowledge, each soul, in its experiences, releases that wisdom from that spirit; once all the spirits fuse again, the nothing will be perfect. And all of that will take place in an instant of the eternity of eternities.

The spirits fused with the souls migrate with each incarnation, teaching new souls how to remember; there are souls with old spirits, which have moved forward in the different incarnations, these vibrate in different scales; they have wisdom, and are familiar with the paths of life and death.

The spirits, the shadows and the entities float between two worlds; once a couple is attracted to each other, their vibrations emit a call that captivates certain souls; in all couples there is always the possibility of a pregnancy; the Moirai, the Fates, provoke that these destinies cross to have one body for one soul.

Before the body exists, the soul vibrates touching those souls, men a women dreaming of children; subtle signals of powerful attraction are induced…

During the pregnancy, there are souls, entities, beings from the underworld, trapped souls that wish to incarnate; no one can imagine the events that take place before an incarnation.

The shadows protect the soul that is going to incarnate; they encapsulate it close to the body it is going to inhabit; once that body is born and detaches from the mother, the incarnation begins; it is something that will take a while.

Every one could remember that moment, that is recorded, the following time; the soul keeps touch with the protective beings; mysterious doors are opened, pets feel them, and incarnated souls smile.

How long do shadows, or those beings known as magical, take care or the souls?

They stay for all their life, but their presence is minimized with time; they don't interfere with actions, they are there, they are voices you hear when you are talking to yourself; they are mute witnesses of that evidence; they are present and are the cause of many events considered miraculous.

You can contact them, communicate with them, feel their presence and know they are there; you do it when you understand the value of life.

Silently, without interfering with your life, without becoming present, they talk to you, inspire you, guide you, they make you change your mind, or your decision; you might have a trip, and something tells you not to go, and you are saved from death.

You go to a place, and something makes you change the course, and in that change, you find the happiness you so longed for; they don't interfere in your decisions, but they insinuate; you are never alone while you are incarnated; they are always there; invite them into your life, and you will understand it.

If the nothing already has everything, why do souls incarnate?

In the earthly world, everything has spirit, some are and remain that way; they don't have one soul, they have many; but everything has a vibration, each plant, insect, stone, water, animal has a unique vibration; it doesn't move forward, it is, and will continue to be through time; its presence complements the mission of the souls, it is part of the self discovering of wisdom.

Those souls don't incarnate, they are perpetual as long as the earth exists; once the earth dies, they will die with it.

Each soul, in its progress and knowledge releases, thru the incarnations, the internal wisdom; most of them don't complete their mission, they must incarnate time and time again until they find the path to freedom.

In creation, my shadows left the guiding principles for each soul to find the path, but freedom has annulled the old knowledge, the souls get lost abandoning the sense of living.

Despite the fact that there are guide entities, shadows and beings of light and darkness that show the way, few souls listen to them.

Occasionally, you need several incarnations in order to finish releasing knowledge. What you are able to do in a lifetime; you could need a thousand lives if you don't know how to act.

In its interior power, the nothing must know the experiential meaning of all the options, and these, take place in each destiny; at the same time, the destiny is in each soul incarnated, and all of them are different.

Imagine the magnitude of wisdom. Millions of lives in eons would just be the beginning of the great knowledge.

The nothing possess all the wisdom, condensed in itself, it must be freed in order to understand it; it is just like a book, you have it in your hands, there is the knowledge, but, the only way to discover it is to read it, each page, an incarnation.

You won't know what the seed is, even though it has all the information; just the fruit will tell which is its essence.

In order to be everything, the nothing discovers itself thru the souls; each soul will have to become the creator of its world, and allow its creations to develop their knowledge; in other words, infinite universes are created within the nothing, within each soul that creates its world; the souls created in said underworld will create another, and another, and another, and so on through eternity; wisdom is infinite in order to reach perfection.

If you are the first creation, do you have a soul? How is the soul of death?

In essence, I am life; I am a part of the spirit; I don't have a soul, I am, like the nothing, the only thing eternal. I am the last thing to come into the repose of existence, and the first thing to wake up; without me, Death, there is no life.

CHARLAS CON LA MUERTE

מדבר עם המוות

I don't have a soul, but I know them all; they live and die, thru me; they transmute in the different incarnations, fulfill destinies, and reach wisdom.

I have seen each soul live and die; I have seen, with sadness, how a life is dilapidated, which shakes my existence.

Do you suffer? Cry?

I have no feelings, I am not corporeal, but I cry when I have to free souls that had empty lives; when a child is murdered or an elderly dies, someone who didn't do a thing in life; it hurts; the impotence produced by seeing abandoned lives, wasted opportunities; either by the hand of a murderer, or by negligence.

There are millions of souls waiting for the opportunity to incarnate; for others who have had it and waste it.

The fantastic experience of living, with all its apparent suffering; to be able to discover the honeys of love; to taste the bitter failure and to find the sweet nectar of triumph. To live is the freedom of being. To complete the task and execute it; a live well lived; these are incarnations that make a difference.

ויקה

Who, or what, defines the mission of the souls?

There isn't a who; the mission of each soul is defined by itself; the essence of the wisdom is concentrated in each spirit; with each different incarnation, you release that wisdom; that way, each life allows you to discover a little more.

Remember, all souls that share a time and a space are linked; they generate bonds that last in time for new souls that will incarnate, each act, no matter how trivial it seems, affects the lives of every one.

See how the development isn't only material, but also spiritual; the incarnation of the souls have created futures and there are infinite futures.

CHARLAS CON LA MUERTE

מדבר עם המוות

You choose your mission thru incarnations, according to the knowledge you have released in each one of them.

When you have a problem, when you have a doubt, when you must find a solution, when you must fulfill a need; you meditate, you enter the mind that joins the spirit and begin the process searching for answers.

All the answers are inside you, it is there where you discover the wisdom; that, you teach to others who gather it along with their progress, and these, to others; eternal wisdom has no end, until you can create your multiverses.

That something that only a few can understand, old spirits, in the progress of the different incarnations, discovers the power of creation, and the first thing they create is death.

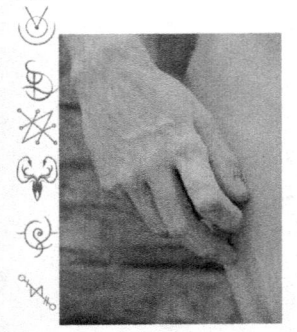

The great sculptor that wants to create his masterpiece, which already exists in his mind, extracted from his inside knowledge, knows that inside the marble block lay all the possible sculptures.

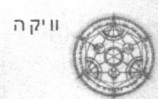

ויקה

It is when he carefully destroys, kills, the pieces of marble that trap the sculpture, and everyone has died that, from within, emerges the creation. The sculpture was always there, trapped.

The same happens with lives, everything is inside each person; you only have to brush away what is left thru the incarnations.

At the end of the path, when you take a look at what you have lived, you can, terrifyingly, see how little you have done in life; a life thrown away, compliant, empty and senseless.

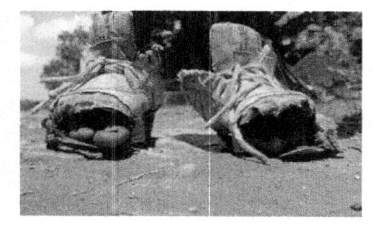

Misused freedom, fear, bad education, culture and dogmas; harsh environments, pleasing parents, are many of the things that can annul progress; they rob the opportunity to discover the potential of interior wisdom.

How do you extract that wisdom?

Through time, while being incarnated in the world of options, each soul discovers itself and discovers the power. Incarnated souls ignore that they inhabit an illusory world that can be modified, transformed or varied.

Some understand it, others suppose it, but few master it.

In the experiences, an infinite number of situations are presented; a mind game, a feeling, an apparent suffering, a need to fulfill.

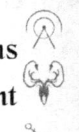

While free, souls act in different ways when face with the same situation; those who seek answers or solutions go on extracting the wisdom they possess. It is just, through the inner search to act on the outside, that you discover yourself, but the mind creates limitation and disability barriers, you see life as a punishment, a destruction, it is cursed, you feel the impotence before the different situations; your will vanishes before the unexpected.

You fall into laziness, conformity, acceptance; the incarnation looses its sense; and empty and useless life.

You live in a world where there is more success that failure, where options are endless; since birth, you have all the solutions and all the answers to all the tests in life.

In you, and within you, the knowledge to sort life is latent, but that knowledge is fragmented in different souls; you need all of them to complete your mission.

You can have the knowledge to sail the seas, but you don't do it alone; you need the carpenter to design the vessel you want, you need the cook to prepare your food; you need the person who knows how to make rope and sails; and if you look closely, you need everyone.

Each one is an expert in their area; they have extracted that specific knowledge so you can complete your mission; and, you help them complete theirs.

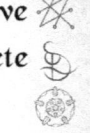

Do you have a problem? If it isn't in you to solve it, someone has it very closely; also, you have the solution that someone might need.

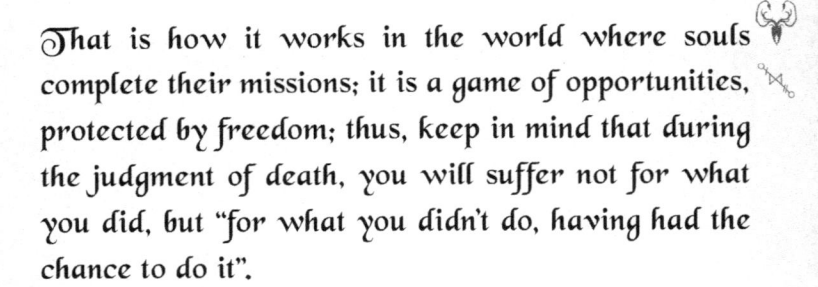

That is how it works in the world where souls complete their missions; it is a game of opportunities, protected by freedom; thus, keep in mind that during the judgment of death, you will suffer not for what you did, but "for what you didn't do, having had the chance to do it".

All events, no matter how simple they might be, are an incredible opportunity to extract your wisdom.

- You can create something new, that everyone needs, and fill a need.
- You can improve or repair something.
- You are a solution for many other questions.
- Before you exist, you are provided with a deep specific knowledge, a gift, an art, a skill; everyone has those tools; they only have to discover them.

Life brings you:

- 💀 Problems
- 💀 Suffering
- 💀 Difficulties
- 💀 Anguish
- 💀 Sorrow
- 💀 Diseases
- 💀 Disappointment & Failure
- 💀 Tragedies
- 💀 Obstacles

The most difficult obstacles, the limitations and the most intense torments; everything your imagination can think of as difficult, unacceptable and tragic.

But, all of that and more is what makes you discover your power; none of that is everlasting, nothing is fixed and can be changed.

When you have a problem, every problem brings you a benefit, but if you learn not to see the problem but the challenge to find solutions, then you'll discover how much you know; and, if you find a solution, the more solutions you find, then you'll realize there is no problem you can't face.

Then your life will have been lived, you'll notice once you face your judgment; that you have progressed in knowledge and wisdom, preparing your next incarnation.

It usually happens that, in several moments of your life, you must face difficult situations, fights, annoyance, abandonment; events that will force your soul to the deepest part of your being; you will feel like you are about to succumb; and when you reach that crucial end, that is when you free the great power you posses; sometimes, it is the only way to realize how strong you are.

WHAT YOU LEAVE IN THE WORLD

This is a part of your judgment, maybe the part that marks your next incarnation. When you die, what did you leave of yourself in the world you are abandoning?

Not just a fleeting memory in those who knew you; what did you improve, create, what is left of you. Which was your contribution to the lives of all the souls?

Did you plant a tree that is now leafy for birds to seek refuge, and lovers to find eternal love?

Which were your actions? Were you of help, or a burden; solution or a problem; did you built or destroy?

It isn't about preserving your name, or your identity; it is about the energies you have left of your presence in the world; maybe, no one knows it, but you do.

You'll understand in the judgment of death.

Once disincarnated, all souls must leave the world with something better than when they found it; they must leave a path, and there is no small path; something from what you've done; if you did it, it will be a contribution for other souls, but what if you didn't do it, having the chance to do it?

What use would your presence have been for?

To leave the world with the knowledge, without taking or leaving anything, is a wasted incarnation; for the departed, for those who stay and for those who will incarnate.

In spite of the apparent problems and suffering, your life is a wonderful experience; it tests you, it makes you strong, it discovers you, and thru you, the power of the spirit discovers itself.

There are no empty lives, only limited minds, blinded by fears, trapped in the dogmas, limited by impoverished cultures of nonexistent precepts.

Life is the variety that offers you all the difficulties, so you can free all the options, you make the change, if you are in this world, and you are here because you have the power to transform it.

Your actions, your thoughts turned into works, your presence; transform worlds; in your freedom you must discover your power, which gift has been given to you; which tool is hidden by your spirit, so you can be part of the change. It is your freedom. Speak to

CHARLAS CON LA MUERTE

מדבר עם המוות

your soul; listen to the shadows that yell at you each dawn...

What have you done with your life? What have you accomplish in your life? There is still time to do it.

How do I know what is my mission?

All incarnations release infinite knowledge that transcend in different lives.

But you forget the passed ones; when you are born, you don't know what is inside of you; you arrive with a seed, and you'll only discover it thru difficulties and needs.

You only take knowledge to the other live, not memories... But you take something else, something that allows you to recognize your mission; that for what you are made for.

- What are you passionate about?
- What do you like?
- What do you dream of when your mind wanders?
- What attracts you the most, and what completes you?

ויקה

What are you good for?

Where do you think you get your taste from, what attracts you; that which flows from your inner self, that which makes you happy. From the depths of incarnations, your soul is filled with that knowledge that transcends in desires; a limitless passion, something that powerfully attracts you.

A gift, a skill, a way of thinking, a trend, and all those virtues are accompanied and attached to a body in which they can flow.

The long and slender fingers of a musician; the fragile and agile body of a dancer, the hands of a sculptor, the strength of a fighter, the calm of a thinker, the curiosity of the discoverer, the devotion to help of the healer; the smell and amazing taste of who loves to cook.

The spatial vision of the architect, the mysterious attraction of the astronomer who seeks the remote space where life began.

All souls are equipped with skills and memories of the knowledge from other lives; they enter the bodies that vibrate with that knowledge; after following it slowly, with time and your passion, your mission is over; although it can happen that you don't realize it.

You'll only understand it at the judgment of death; live, built, follow your dreams and your passion; that way, your life will be complete.

Your achievements will be easier, you'll discover the sense of "being alive" once you do what you love; you discover why you are here.

Your actions will affect all the souls, in one way or another; those who live with you, as well as the ones that are yet to come.

But you must take the time to look inside a soul; freedom makes many to follow dreams from others; or to limit theirs; the soul gets confused with the different alternatives of life; the wrong decisions are made, you do what you don't have to, and act on what you don't want, where there is no passion or desire.

To live without it, is to live an empty life that will soon fall into the routine and the grief; it provided nothing, it gives nothing; and, there is nothing at the time of your death; you stopped doing what could've been done.

Your mission is within you, but not as you perceive it from the world of the living; you have a destiny that you are building, and in that destiny, you come across with other destinies throughout your life; and at the same time with others; between one and others, the Moirai will help you to complete your mission.

Which can be completed in many ways, or actions that you will probably ignore, but you are in the world for a reason, it will transcend in the futures; all souls are intertwined.

Who controls the destinies? Who are the Moirai?

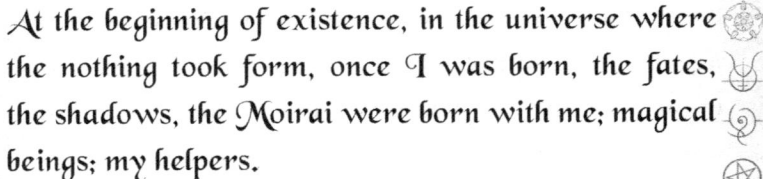

At the beginning of existence, in the universe where the nothing took form, once I was born, the fates, the shadows, the Moirai were born with me; magical beings; my helpers.

They are present thru all the experiences of the souls, they act in silence; you perceive them and feel them, they guide or impulse your life in different ways.

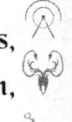

Them, and myself; we take care of each soul, but we deeply respect freedom; we are inspiration, give signals, block decisions so you don't fall and loose your way; we show you the path, and if you invoke us, and allow our guidance, you'll feel our presence.

We are present in all human cultures, as a memory; we are ignored as something existent, but we are real, we run the threads of life.

The Moirai, my sisters, provide you with these strange elements that go by with no reason; you live in misfortune and, suddenly, without knowing how, happiness arrives.

You have a need, and in some strange way, your destiny changes finding a solution; luck and destiny are deeply related; luck is given to you by my sisters; and me, with one of them, we give you life and death.

Keep it in mind during your journey thru life; you'll never be alone; remember that there is a fragile line between both worlds, where the souls connect and the spirits flow; that metaphysic immaterial world in which you can enter, if you know the secrets to do it.

We've been forgotten, distorted our existence; we've been condemned as the destructors of life, cruel and malevolent; they've created gods that usurp our presence; but, there are still the arcana to find the pacts and invoke our presence.

If you know how to do it, if you listen in the silence of your soul; if you watch the signs, if you understand and commit yourself to live; don't doubt it, we'll be by your side so you can complete your mission, and your life will be complete for your next incarnations.

But you will always be free to invoke us or forget about us; maybe you'll know during the judgment of death, if you didn't do, having had the chance to do it.

Since ancient times in the world of the living, the Moirai, the Fates, have always existed; they are not a legend, they are real; and death is the only sure thing you have in life.

But, we don't act unless invoked, just as you look for food in the physical world, that is how you must do it in the spirit world; we are so close, and so far at the same time; it is up to you, if you want, to know me and discover life.

But you will feel our presence in unimaginable ways; wonderful things will happen, you'll have a destiny without obstacles, if you let yourself be guided; you'll have inspirations that shall be your luck to help you complete your mission; we're not you enemies, nor the destruction; we just take care of souls that incarnate and disincarnate for their path thru eternity. We are the fates; we are death and life.

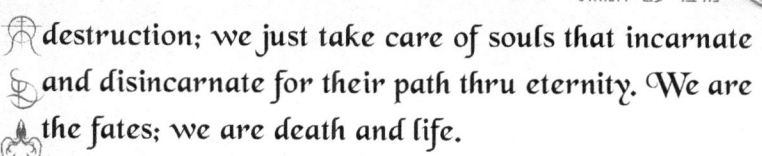

How can one live fully and complete the mission? You are death, your secrets, left by the shadows don't exist, as you say; they are just vague memories of philosophies or cultures already gone. How should I live so, at the time of the judgment, I can complete my mission?

The process of life is a fantastic adventure for the souls; you are born in a body, a place, with a culture, a language, and an unknown world; at the beginning you won't understand you are there, and why you are there.

In your childhood you are not you; even though you've already shown your gifts and your skills; it will be up to your guides, your parents, educators, culture; whether these gifts are exalted, encouraged or annulled, something that happens to most; it is where you see those who triumph since they are young and those who fail.

The soul gifted with the wisdom of artists, is able to express in a wall the first traces of the great painter; there are two destinies, it can be supported, encouraged, allowed; or it is punished annulling the virtue.

You must face the whim of those who protect your small body; the imposition of what others want you to be; they take away your dreams and amputate your mission.

Most of the souls get lost at the beginning of their incarnations; dogmas, creeds, believes, and cultures drown the knowledge that transcends from other lives, they condemn it, question it, judge it and lastly, they destroy it bringing the souls to the unhappiness of a life; they last in time where, maybe, the inner power is allowed in a given moment in their freedom.

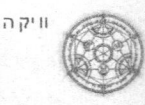

Have you seen how children are taught not to built, to fight for their ideals; but it is always imposed; they are taught that their life is just what a god will want; that they have to ask said god; that said god is in charge; children are limited, their dreams are torn, their existence is torn to pieces before they even know it.

They are imposed on without allowing their essence to flow; ignorant guides, their ignorance destroys souls and incarnations; that is why you see living bodies without souls, everywhere.

Beings lost in their inner misery, empty lives, isolated from the real meaning, sanctimonious people who pray to a god for the solution, when all the solutions are in their soul; these are beings that in their judgment, when they die, will understand that they had everything, but the fear for their believes drowned them.

Just when the final moment comes, death comes. When they die, some see in fear that their life was useless.

CHARLAS CON LA MUERTE

מדבר עם המוות

With childhood comes rebellion; you fight for that desire that you bring from other lives, the restlessness, the tendency where you perceive the fulfillment with what you do; that who discovers that treasure and find support grows in their passion, living life in full joined, forever, by luck.

We always leave a guide to understand the souls; a way to find incarnated spirits and help them in their new incarnation but, with time, dogmas and whims succumbed freedom into the slavery of spirits.

When a soul incarnates, set it free, observe what skill it has, allow its insides to flow, that which shows, encourage it, help it grow; that way it will be easier to find its path. Don't corrupt it, or impose. Take care of it; support that soul once you discover its gift and its wisdom. You will be proud of your children,

ויקה

and you'll see that in your judgment. It isn't what you want for your children, it is what their spirits want to be.

In spite of that, the Moirai and my helpers will modify the destinies so that those souls can find their path; that is why, sometimes, souls find their passion after several apparent sufferings and difficulties.

If you watch carefully, the ones that suffer the most are those who don't do what they want; those who are imposed, whose opportunities of being are closed, and the spirit fights in spite of that; it isn't that hard, you just have to observe and see around you; not the bodies, but the souls trapped in senseless lives.

If you dare to ask, you'll understand the pain of many who live lives they don't want to live.

They had opportunities, they are incarnated in the world of options, millions of alternatives to free their wisdom but were lives cut short, senseless. What do they bring to the other life? What did they leave in this one? What did they do in their live, and what did they stop doing? Nothing...

They want me as a balm to heal their empty lives, thinking, wrongly, that they'll free from their sorrows but... On the contrary, they will face the worst of judgments...

But everyone can change, if you change the perspective and break the bonds that control you, you must do it in time; if you let the opportunity pass you by, your life would have been in vane. You'll suffer a thousand incarnations for what you left undone, having had the chance to do it.

It could be difficult at first, but if you really want a change, my allies will help you; it could be hard.

You'll face your acts, after your death, so think well how you live while you live.

LIFE

Wake up every morning, discover the power within you, understand that your days under the sun are brief; your existence travels, every second, to the ends of the afterlife.

Don't stop for temporary sufferings, get over them, discover your inner strength and, rise above adversity; within you, deep inside your being, there are all the answers, and the options are in the earthly world.

Be happy, but push yourself in order to achieve it, don't fall into temporary and useless well-being; fight with all your might to conquer each day.

In spite of the haze, the sun continues its path thru your life; stay away from evil, whenever you can, but always give the best of you.

Torments come from your mind, not your life, and they'll live in there as long as you want, and allow, them to; rip them out, act, revitalize your existence, live each day as it was your last day.

Achieve your goals, no matter how hard they are, you'll be able to reach them if you really decide to.

Follow your dreams, fight for them, be the creator of your destiny, don't let yourself be discouraged by the unexpected, don't succumb to adversity; it is in your life to challenge you, defy you, so you can demonstrate how great you are, or so you can be defeated without trying.

Watch your actions, do what you must do, but be aware of the consequences, appreciate your life and your pleasures while you have them; enjoy your skin and the earth, you only have one chance, don't waste it in failed dreams.

You can do it, if you really want it!

Tell me about love

What is to love?

It is a deep feeling, the force that moves the souls; a bond that lasts beyond life, when you really love.

To love, causes the most agonic pain, so intense that it fragments the spirits after death; some for eternity.

Love is the feeling that possesses time; the utmost happiness, and the most terrible destruction of the soul.

To love is the act that destroys more lives, and the more condemned during the judgment of death.

When you love, if you don't do it with love, you not only damage you body, you damage life, you cut dreams and illusions, destroy hopes; you throw into the fire of doubt the fear, the abandonment, the misfortune, and who suffers for love.

Love is the living essence, is the union of two souls that build new paths where they'll give life to the souls they incarnate; it's the feeling that frees the strength of the spirit to live.

Love moves you, uplifts you, enlarges you, makes you superior and moves the threads of life to meet goals and realizations; love builds the destinies of two into one.

But, when you cause pain for love, when you cover other interests, when you lie and cheat, when you just presume to submit or attain; when you lie to yourself, not loving who you say to love; then you destroy, and destroy yourself.

Maybe you don't realize it, and presume of the feats of love, maybe you ignore the damage caused and forget about it, but you'll remember it, and see the fruit of your actions.

Many souls incarnated in bodies torn by shattered love; you don't destroy a person, you destroy thousands; abandoned children, without guidance or food; suffering mothers, betrayed fathers, tarnished lives.

Love is something you must manage with sincerity, honesty, respect and dignity.

Love without possession, without waiting; love without understanding destiny and love; just love.

Don't use love as an excuse to live, don't hide behind false love; be love; live love freely; remember that a

A feeling so deep, transcends incarnations or fragments and destroys spirits, souls and bodies; its up to you.

If you have love debts, it is time to pay them, for you and for those who are suffering because of you.

Don't love with a hidden agenda, be cautious, take some time before loving and giving your body, and your destiny, away; remember that the bonds of love are eternal through the incarnations, and, if you truly love, love will follow you in other lives; you'll feel it, don't ever doubt it.

Don't suffer for love, you'll live much heartbreak; you'll be disappointed, but what is important isn't the love they offer you; what is truly valuable is the love you have to give.

Control love, always; if you let it free, it will drag you to dark worlds from which you won't be able to scape; you'll make mistakes for love; mistakes that will destroy your live, and even your incarnations.

Take care of your skin, it is the temple of your spirit; don't tarnish it disguising your carnal desires as love;

enjoy your desire, but don't shield it or mislead it with a fictional love.

Love is the most sublime expression of the life and gratitude of the souls; treasure and respect it.

True love and passion are the engines to reach your dreams.

How should I act?

There is no code or laws that you have to obey, you are free to act, or not; it is up to you, but you must be prepared.

The anxiety of life will take you thru arid paths; doubts and uncertainty will trap your mind, disorienting you.

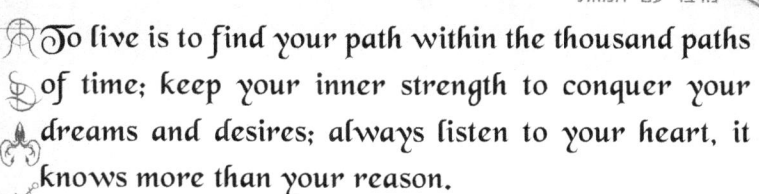

To live is to find your path within the thousand paths of time; keep your inner strength to conquer your dreams and desires; always listen to your heart, it knows more than your reason.

Value your life as the dearest possession; live freely without altering the life of others, or seeing the freedom of others; each one lives their experience as they choose.

Try with all your might to fight a little more, each day; push yourself, know, learn, face adversity with dignity, not with weakness; discover the path that takes you to the limit of comfort.

You are the builder of your live, you create the paths of your destiny; each path has two edges, always walk in the center.

Don't let yourself get carried away by senseless affairs, or walk in a path that doesn't belong to you; don't follow other footprints, or try to have others follow yours; be prudent in your actions and when speaking.

The door to your life must, always, be very small, so that only those who can help you grow can enter; stay away from arrogance, vanity, trickery; learn to be at peace, look for the serenity of your mind, and you'll have serenity in your soul.

Remember that it is your life, and your destiny; learn not to damage other destinies intervening in them, even if you think your are right; educate, teach, show how a path is built, but never build one that isn't yours.

You live with a universe of souls that vibrate in different scales, some will want to trap you, others to condemn you; always, look for the intensions, and take some time to ponder.

There isn't a life without penury, challenges, happiness and infidelity; your life is an event hive that sways between the calm and the storm; learn to navigate in it.

Every sunset, take a moment to heal your soul and evaluate your acts; every day, review your new path; always keep in your memory that, no matter what you do, that won't condemn you, but always think in what you leave undone.

Whatever you do is done, and you will have to answer for it, but you will be sorry for what you didn't do, having had the chance to do it.

Try to meet your goals, fight for your dreams, that which you bring from other incarnations; that mysterious something that is your deepest desire; fight to conquer it, trust in the beings that watch for your destiny, seek them, invoke them, invite them to your live so they become beacons during nights of confusion. Soon you'll realize that you can move forward and transform your life.

Watch for lost souls, they can seek your downfall; stay away from temptations that seem to take you to fortune and glory; they are paths that lead to pain and suffering.

Allow each one to live their life, freely; don't compete with others in life; someday, everyone will die.

Don't become to attached to anything from the earthy world; everything is temporary, enjoy it to the fullest while you posses it; use it, make it work for you to fulfill your dreams and complete your mission, but don't create bonds with earth; when you die, none of

CHARLAS CON LA MUERTE

your possessions can come with you; your body and all material possessions are from the earth, and they will stay in it.

If you keep ties with what you could no longer have, then your spirit will fragment, you can turn into a ghost trapped between life and death for something that you could never have for eternity.

Don't damage your incarnations accumulating dirt, you can't bring it with you; what is from the earth, is of the earth; others will enjoy what you can't.

Lean out and watch, the hands of time move in reverse, your time in this world can end, at any second. Think of what is left for you to do?

Which task you still have to conclude? Which is the hug you have denied, and still have to give?

When we meet, face to face, in the judgment of life, remember that what hurts the most will be what you left undone, not what you did...

You have something to do, live your life to the fullest, and do what you must, without destroying you time.

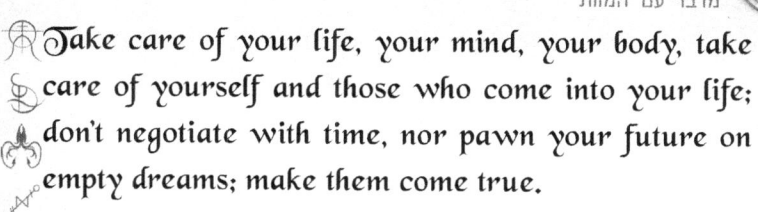

Take care of your life, your mind, your body, take care of yourself and those who come into your life; don't negotiate with time, nor pawn your future on empty dreams; make them come true.

Learn from the experience you get from failures, learn from your errors and mistakes, don't remain trapped in the difficult moments, nor presume of overcoming them; always remember that life is changing, everything comes and goes, the storms appear without warning, prepare yourself to learn how to enter and scape from them.

When someone dies, don't tear yourself apart for those who leave; let them go, now that you understand the migration of the souls.

That's why you must be at peace with everyone around you, no one knows when is their time, nor where or when their souls must leave; learn to discover the value of life from those that are with you; you won't do it later.

There will come a day, an instant, where you'll feel that your world is covered by an unimaginable

CHARLAS CON LA MUERTE

מדבר עם המוות

darkness; your senses will freeze, you'll feel a deep nothing in your soul, a mix of pain and impotence.

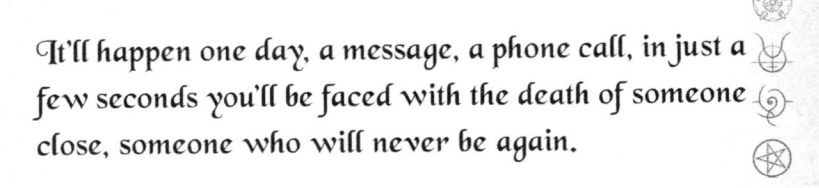

It'll happen one day, a message, a phone call, in just a few seconds you'll be faced with the death of someone close, someone who will never be again.

You'll see their body withered, lifeless, you'll be able to talk to them, yell at them, you'll be able to do what you want, but that lifeless body will not hear you.

Only the darkness will take over your mind and your heart, you'll feel sorrow, pain and a profound sadness.

You can avoid all that if you understand this today, and act in a certain way so, if someone dies, you can understand that they begin a journey to new incarnations, another adventure of life; they were the best, gave their best; and there was nothing left to do.

You mustn't pray to the dead, or impose on them tasks they can't complete; the dead are dead; you are alive.

They don't need anything from you, or anything you do can reach them; there is no use for masses, prayers,

A requiem, burials or visits to the cemetery; they are earth that goes back to the earth; if you want to do something, do it for the living; the dead are meant to be forgotten, by you; when they die, they break all bonds with life.

Whenever possible, try to understand instead of being understood, and always, try to be at peace, with yourself and with those around you. But, don't allow other to take advantage of you because of your feelings.

You don't have to be a slave of other lives, simply do what you want to do.

DECISIONS

Your life and your destiny are the fruit of your decisions; you walk the path and you are free to do it.

You build the path of existence; in every step you take moved by a decision; your decision.

Life is the path of a thousand paths, you must, always, think and act with caution; you are entwined with all the souls sharing your incarnation, in one way or

CHARLAS CON LA MUERTE

מדבר עם המוות

another destinies intertwine; that's why you must be ware of which path you're going to take.

It is in you to move the threads of your live according to your desires; you have everything, and can obtain everything; you give, and you receive what you really want; nothing and no one sets limits to your spirit, only you can do it.

Or you can be the creator of fantastic universes if you make decisions wisely, intertwining with one and other; for that, you must think, meditate, and analyze before you act.

Your thinking is the architect that builds the path, in everything there is, in love, success, triumph and the unavoidable failure.

What happens in your life and in your future is solely your fault, you have the freedom to choose between one destiny and the other; if you defy life, and you venture daringly thru forbidden paths; you'll suffer.

But, if you are alive, you can correct your path and, with the same decisions plus the experience you have, you can rise above adversity, no matter how difficult

ויקה

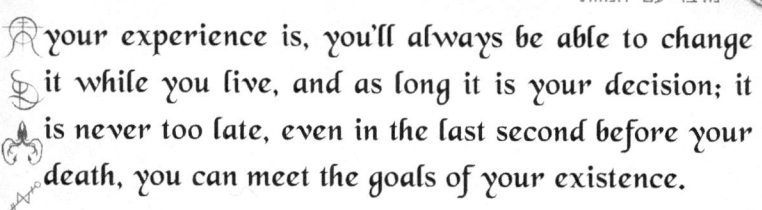

As your experience is, you'll always be able to change it while you live, and as long it is your decision; it is never too late, even in the last second before your death, you can meet the goals of your existence.

In the loneliness of your mind, find your power, don't win in the face of adversity; it is something fleeting that allows you to extract the great knowledge that is in you.

You'll face difficult times, obstacles, barriers, criticism, disdain, betrayals, and deceptions; time and time again you'll be faced with the darkness of your soul.

Through your life, you'll know the different pains and heartaches; you'll walk thru the valley of the bones and the thorns that will drill your heart, taking your conscience to unreason bordering on madness.

You'll feel desperate, sad and overwhelmed, you'll invoke me, many times as a way out from your suffering; and others, you'll want to die.

For that you have to prepare yourself, you have to walk the paths of fire that will cool down your spirit, don't rush yourself, you won't have what you can't handle.

Regardless of the disguise of life, it will always be to extract the strength from within; and it will depend on you, and only you, how you use it.

As long as you are alive, you'll always be able to change the course of your destiny, even in the last second before your death.

Everything you experience in life will depend on the decisions you make; it is only up to you; think well before you act; look for my allies for guidance, make a pact of life with me; if you do it, I'll take your hand to guide you.

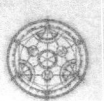

You must remember that it'll not be my voice that you hear, my signs are events that take place to guide you; when something doesn't go as you planned, look at the sign telling you you've been saved... my hand will show you, in time, what you were saved from.

I will be there, every day; not so you die, but so you live to the fullest.

Tell me about the process of incarnation. How is a mission chosen? How do you come back to life? Where do you incarnate? Can you go back to the same place, with the same people?

The life you abandoned is forgotten, you won't remember how or where you came from; none of that will be kept in your soul, but the knowledge and the wisdom, tastes, desires, wishes, what you are passionate about, that will transcend; that will mark your spirit for eternity, and that which has emerged from your spirit, you'll take to your incarnations.

Time doesn't exist in the spirit as in does in the spaces, you can incarnate in the same place and at the same time where you just died, nothing prevents it.

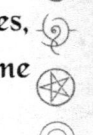

You can incarnate at any time in any space, since your mind is empty of memories, you'll adapt to this reality; as time passes by, your inner knowledge and yourself can begin to flow.

The souls float waiting for a body, it is the most traumatic part of the incarnation; the soul feels attracted to an empty body and incarnates in it; the souls don't enter during gestation; there can't be two souls living in the same body.

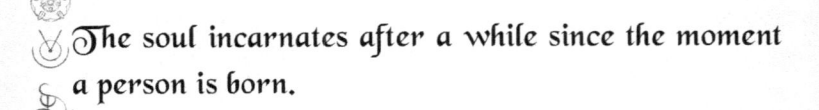

The soul incarnates after a while since the moment a person is born.

That is when destinies open, and it's there where the most important thing is the responsibility for the children.

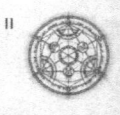

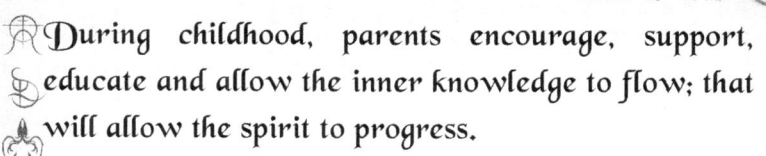

During childhood, parents encourage, support, educate and allow the inner knowledge to flow; that will allow the spirit to progress.

But, if these are controlling parents, they impose, punish, reprimand; they can even destroy a valuable incarnation.

A person is born with incredible abilities, has knowledge from lives, and that knowledge flows in their actions.

Their clean mind is ready to know and understand the world where they incarnated; during their childhood they can learn many languages, can develop great innate skills that came with its spirit, as tools.

But, if the body incarnated is in a difficult and hostile environment, it will be very hard to complete their mission.

Millions of boys and girls are abused, abandoned, subdued, controlled, and battered by irresponsible and miserable parents that impose dogmas, creeds, limitations, punishments and misfortune on them, destroying not only their tender body, but the profound opportunity a spirit has to provide knowledge when it incarnates.

In the judgment of death, when I face those who destroyed the lives and souls of the innocents, they pay a price in the afterlife, where they'll relive their actions for eternity.

They will have to see, time and time again, what that person would have done, what he would have contributed, but wasn't allowed to live.

Who gives life, builds a temple for the soul to inhabit, and must know what a responsibility a child is.

But not only for a body, but for the development of the souls; no one is born bad, perverse or destructive; if the knowledge brought form other lives isn't channeled, the soul rebels, gets confused, altered and looses its course.

It is when the mind transforms, rebellion makes way to violence, the soul struggles in the darkness to find the path, but many never find it, even though they want to.

A person educated in the limitation, the abuse, and the violence, will only give abuse and violence; a person, who is motivated, and supported, discovers their skills, and if these are channeled since childhood, they will have many triumphs.

There are no destructive souls, there are energetic souls, with a lot of strength, who can build and destroy; it depends on the guides of its childhood.

Even with this, each soul has the freedom to change and transform its destiny, just in the doorstep of the afterlife you understand how that freedom makes you loose so many incarnations; when you loose the sense of life in banalities or you loose the sense of being.

If the world understood the true value of death, it would value life to the fullest, but there is the secret, you must ignore what happens to be completely free.

There is no return of the dead, life doesn't end with death; nothing really dies, it only transforms and the souls are eternal.

How can you help those souls so they can complete their mission in this world?

When a soul incarnates, it gives signs of what it brings with it; you must learn to feel with your soul, observe, be aware; slowly you'll understand that that person has skills, tastes; they will be more attracted to some things, and they will ignore others.

Since their mind is empty, fill it with knowledge, show them the world, but allow them to choose what attracts them from it, don't deny or prevent them, don't channel their mind to your desires; let them act.

Educate them without controlling them, give them natural elements to act with, be patient; once you understand your desires and their innate skills, encourage them, guide them, soon you'll realize the power they have.

Remember that the souls, when incarnated, don't know laws or rules to live; it must be taught, discipline and constancy, allow them to discover solutions, let them grow independently, but feeling your love and your guidance.

Fill their needs, remember that you are responsible for that soul, and that life; when a child is born, an opportunity for an incarnation is also born; don't just look at the material body, look at the essence he has.

Let them grow at their pace, but don't forget to feed their mind; support them in their decisions, they are the seed that emerges from other lives; maybe, that is why you can see the world, how many souls are lost because they don't have the chance to free what they bring with them.

You can see people bitter, unsuccessful, unhappy, filled with a great nothing and pain; inert beings who live without living; watching the days, months and years go by, without achieving anything.

Suffering people where there are no more dreams; they lived the lives and desires of others, they were limited, imposed with knowledge they didn't want; they closed their destinies to submission.

When they die, and are faced with the judgment, they'll understand that that incarnation was lost.

You can also observe how others grow, meet their goals, develop their capabilities at short age, live different lives contributing wisdom and progress to the other souls; that is how they complete their mission.

Life is a maze with many options and great responsibilities, a soul doesn't incarnate if there is no body, and those who conceive the bodies, unfortunately, ignore the souls.

Maybe now that you understand it you can appreciate the magical experience of giving life, the responsibility to educate a soul so it can complete its mission.

Also, each one, after their death will have to face their judgment and there, they will know how much damage they caused, or how supportive was of their children.

Every one is responsible for the souls of every one, they aren't in the same time by chance, but because of the cause that joins them in that discovery.

If you look well, you'll realize; humanity goes at a pace where everyone contributes, all the souls that are born in a certain moment, are compatible with that moment.

They contribute knowledge that improves what is there, progress is multiplied, other gifted souls are born; since childhood they posses skills for the development of what exists.

Each generation that has existed has similar qualities; in the different eras, the souls that must be there are born; in that place, in that instant; they vibrate in the same scale, and the mission of each soul incarnated is to complement the others, to progress in knowledge.

But... Abandonment, a scream, a blow, a denial, a punishment, a look down, or an insult that minimizes the dignity, will make everything difficult, very difficult for that soul.

Unfortunately in this world, this happens to most people; the ancient knowledge about the progress of the soul is lost; maybe now the value of life will be understood.

Many, for being free since early age, reach greater progress than those who live under submission.

CHARLAS CON LA MUERTE

מדבר עם המוות

You must allow them and encourage them since their youth, emancipate them, educate them to be independent; with that freedom, they'll be able to extract their knowledge, the soul will flow before the need and the apparent suffering.

They will have the freedom to build the destiny they want, they will sail thru the times and will understand the line that divides happiness from unhappiness.

- Will discover love and sorrow
- Will discover triumph and failure
- Feel the fear that will make them brave
- Know the ends of freedom
- Learn from their mistakes
- Learn from their good choices
- Will discover the souls of the others
- Will create universes where to built their world
- Will conceive bodies that will nestle new souls

But you always have to be there to support them, never to be the savior of their mistakes.

You'll never be able to heal the broken heart, but you can give a comforting embrace.

ויקה

Having children is to open the doors to the spiritual world for souls to incarnate.

Educate them, teach them and prepare them to be independent, and not to be submissive, companions and slaves.

Also, you must be prepared, since their birth, to let them go, you must always be prepared for the farewells, it doesn't matter how they come; a child who leaves, a love that ends, someone's death.

Those are my disguises, many things die during life; not just the flesh, you must always be prepared for the mutations, the changes that come without warning; that is a task you must teach your children.

How can one handle the feelings to avoid suffering?

You can't avoid suffering, but you can understand it; if you recognize in it the experience you are supposed to learn.

When you suffer your mind gets cloudy and the pain overwhelms you; that discovers you sensibility, your feelings are what make you be, live, share, progress or decline.

But your feelings are your worst enemies, you keep in your soul the ones that produce pain, agony and suffering; that feeling can transcend with you to other incarnations, and maybe other might come with you from past ones.

Dark feelings will damage your destiny if you allow them to nestle in it.

Revenge, hatred, resentment, disdain, envy, and betrayal; everything that can tarnish your soul, slowly destroys your life and the life of others.

You must deal with the events that bring out that feeling; you must learn to understand what you feel and act.

Feelings damage your soul when you accept, say nothing, humble yourself and subdue; they are alive as long as the act that caused them is alive in your mind. That is why you must always be in harmony with yourself, stay away from evil, or you'll die in it.

Avoid negative people that can alter your live, although they are part of your existence and you learn from them, you must know when to ignore them, but don't let this blind you to discover the kindness that exists in each soul.

Create your world, create your destiny, it is the only thing you really possess; be reserved, prudent, use the cunning of instinct to navigate between the destinies that will join yours; search for the mystery of your refuge, there you'll put to the test the tenacity of your spirit.

Live your life intensely, without looking at the world around you or other people's destinies; you'll always find other souls, other destinies in your path; some better or worst than yours, but use this to help you modify your life, or to encourage you to be better.

Don't presume of your success or your good choices, don't celebrate your beginnings, be cautious; you'll attract envy and discord; you can see bodies, but ignore interest and temptations.

Deceit remains in the souls whose destinies have been mistaken; they will torment you trying to possess yours.

Always live your life in the balance between your mind and your spirit, remember that you will see all your actions, as simple as they are, during your judgment; always think very well what you are going to do, evaluate, analyze, don't let yourself be carried away by temporary motivations or momentary interests; push yourself to meet your goals, without being indebted to others. If you do it, those others will be your executioners.

Learn from your experiences, each day; know good and evil; discover the hidden intentions of those around you, learn from them; you'll not only be protected by knowing them, but you'll avoid committing them.

Fight for your life, is the most precious thing you have, avoid war, conflict, and risks to the maximum; don't you dare tempt me in adventurous acts, you'll die if you fail.

You have a mind filled with a spirit of power, you could navigate all the adversities of your existence if you know how to act; but... There will be times where you must fight for your life, and you must do it, you'll be tested in a thousand different ways, time and time again; always prepare yourself to deal with those moments.

Trust your instinct, your body has the ability to perceive the dangers that lie in wait, crunched in the darkness of the unknown, in souls, bodies and even in some places.

When faced by inevitable Fates, be prepared, don't keep anything so you can't be possessed by anything; you'll never be able to have more than nothing.

Some day you'll have to leave everything, but there is also a moment in your life when you can loose it all, but... If you know how to live, and you are alive, you can start over; you can always begin.

Posses what you desire to help you complete your mission and be happy; nothing, and no one can keep you from it, but don't accumulate what you'll have to abandon.

Enjoy your days, your nights; enjoy your pleasures, these are part of your life; enjoy your freedom, but watch that it doesn't damage any other soul; and, if you are doing that, don't contain your desires and

CHARLAS CON LA MUERTE

מדבר עם המוות

whims, but do it with discretion, or you'll awaken the envies that will bring destruction.

As time passes, abandon your yesterday, meet you goals and forget them, acknowledge the cycle of changes; once you acquire more experience, leave your temporary fantasies behind; and the more knowledge you have, and the more you understand the true meaning of life, your existence will be more profound and spiritual.

Adversity will always be there, from the time when you are born; learn to know it, strengthen you mind and your body, you don't now what type of disguise it may wear, or from where it comes from, but when it appears, always think what lesson you must learn.

Don't fight against adversity, you'll fall in useless suffering; you'll always loose to it, but if you are strong, inside, and understand the signs of the universe, walk hand in hand with adversity, let it pass; allow time to dance in your mind while you recover your harmony. Once adversity realizes that you don't despair or alter yourself, or curse, nor struggle trying to avoid it when you are already faced with it; when it has

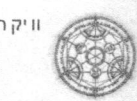

ויקה

nothing else to do, adversity will respect you by not getting closer.

Everything that you came into this world with has a reason, so you can complete a mission; it isn't a punishment if you are handicapped, but it can be something from your other reincarnations.

And are an important part of your mission, whether is to teach, or to learn; to discover a benefit for all souls; look for what your limitations can contribute; yours are not limitations, per se; if you do it carefully, without self hurting you, without cursing, without complaining to life you'll notice that those limitations are a more profound virtue, no one can know the design of the missions of the souls, they each contribute.

Have you seen a child who is born mutilated? How much do they teach? How many will benefit from their presence in this world?

Somewhere else, there is an incarnated soul that needs them like that, mutilated, to design a prosthetic with them that will save the many lives of those who end up mutilated after an accident.

CHARLAS CON LA MUERTE

מדבר עם המוות

The labyrinths of destiny created by my sisters, the Moirai, are unfathomable; it is up to you, how you see your weaknesses; they can be your strength.

WEALTH AND POVERTY

All material things are soil, and belong to the earth; while you live, you can possess all the soil you want in all its possible forms, but avoid the earth from possessing you with its treasures; when you die, and must leave it all behind, your earthly possessions will fragment your spirit.

Wealth is the fruit of your effort, the way you award yourself for achieving your goals, but it isn't a synonym of completing your mission, nor a requirement to do it; it is your freedom to have earth while you are alive, but the wealth of your mind and you soul is more valuable than all the treasures of all the universes.

Wealth brings you benefits, it enlarges you; if you use it wisely it will make others complete their mission; is a chain of growth links; if you use it in arrogance, it will be your destruction.

ויקה

מדבר עם המוות

In order to find wealth, you must push yourself, that will make you extract the knowledge you have in your spirit; and that knowledge helps you to progress in the new incarnations.

You must be prudent, just as wealth brings you benefits, joy and happiness, it can also attract the greatest misfortunes, including your early death.

If you have it, you must use your wealth wisely; remember that you won't be able to bring anything from this world. Avoid leaving wars and destruction after you are gone.

If you are poor, and that is your wish, your experience might be precarious, but you won't have great ties, per se; it isn't much what your really need to live, but extreme poverty can show a void in the spirit to fight; no soul is condemned to suffer deprivation during an incarnation.

Some justify their misery as humility or mystification; it is, in itself, their incapacity to fight; they get used to a world of easy or are waiting for charities; they are beggars of soul, in their freedom, they turn into parasites, they are empty lives... Your presence on

ויקה

earth is to enhance the value of the strong spirit that is inside you, but your mind and your freedom can tarnish it.

Others will suggest you to be unhappy, miserable and unfortunate; to give away the fruit of your labor because, with that, you'll earn heaven after your death.

There is no heaven or hell, nor punishment for being rich or poor; that is your freedom, but, rich or poor, you can complete your mission; you are alive, you have a powerful spirit, it will all depend on what earth you want for your flesh; how do you want to live, and how you live will be your decision. In your judgment, you'll see what you left undone having had the chance to do it for yourself, and for others.

Probably in an earthly world of material philosophies, as a poor person, you'll have to do without many things; that is something you have to think very carefully; diseases, hardship, difficulties, disdain, you'll have to fight harder to survive; maybe, your daily suffering, which was first the motivation for your spirit to unleash its power, in time will end up being what annuls you.

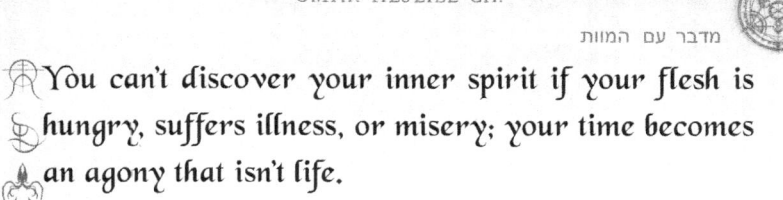

You can't discover your inner spirit if your flesh is hungry, suffers illness, or misery; your time becomes an agony that isn't life.

Remember; poverty in not the absence of wealth, it is also the absence of the strength produced by progress, advance, the development of not only your soul, but of others.

Look at the world. Me, as death, I see with sad eyes how lives are lost, for lack of effort, abused boys and girls, abandoned in misery; children of conformist parents, with impovered minds and dead spirits.

But I've seen many souls emerge from difficulty, souls that leave great works for those who are left behind, and for who will incarnate. When you are rich, you can enjoy the earthly possessions, which, depending on how you use your wealth will be you illumination or your darkness; the Moirai, in their wisdom, allow souls to have, and just look thru the all knowing magic eye, to see what you do with your wealth; maybe the existence of the poor is the test for the souls of the rich.

The rich has; they are trapped with all their wealth, but they can, just like nature, use that wealth and their wisdom to help others reach their happiness.

It isn't to give wealth to the defenseless; that's a mistake; is to create the wheel of life, invest in knowledge, help in education, motivate lives, build paths for others to follow.

A rich person who uses their wealth for their benefit and for others, have the utmost greatness; there is so much to be done, and only a few do it. That's the reason behind the sentence for what you left undone, having had the chance to do it.

Open schools, create businesses and hand them over to others, recycle your money; a rich person who invests so other can start, wins more than money.

מדבר עם המוות

וויקה

CHARLAS CON LA MUERTE

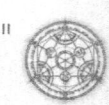

מדבר עם המוות

ויקה

THE CYCLE OF DEATH

While you live, you'll live in the cycle of death; it is constantly there, in nature, to show you the path of life.

If you observe, learn, relate to your life, you can apply it to all your experience, it will help you complete your mission; it is there for you, like an opened book, you just have to look at one page each day.

Everything lives, and everything dies, a little at a time; in an endless cycle of existence where, slowly, the transformation creates the works of existence.

SPRING OF DEATH

Death is the chisel that gives shape to the masterpiece of life; it carves, from the most splendid dawns when the day breaks, to the most beautiful sunsets when the day ends.

You've seen how spring opens the womb of life, creating beautiful colorful landscapes in every corner.

Life is impregnated with the fragrances of life, everything is life, it renews existence, a plethoric moment where harmony dances; the Moirai that rule nature, teach you that there is a season of rejoice and well-being.

That everything is renewed to begin again; that, in spite of the difficult moments where adversity traps you, when the black clouds of the storms in you soul make you doubt life; remember that new springs will come, they always do.

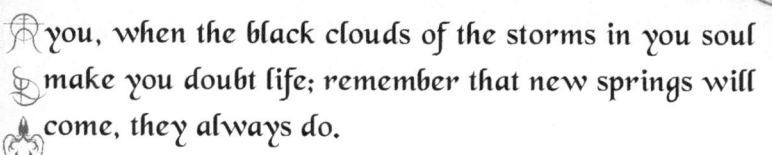

It is the reminder that everything passes, everything changes, all storms pass; you are reminded of the priceless value of being alive. No matter how much you suffer and considered your life to be a disaster, there is always another spring, somewhere in your destiny.

SUMMER OF DEATH

Once something is born, in the same instant, it begins to die; the clever disseat of nature that leads you to the highest end of well-being and happiness.

Intense summers filled with light, life, and joy, where life trusts in life; it takes pleasure in its murmur, without seeing the omen of death.

Intermittent summers dressed in elegance and sumptuousness, are the executioners of your soul, they will test you to the limit; they'll lift you up to let you fall; they'll shake you in the depths of you being.

CHARLAS CON LA MUERTE

מדבר עם המוות

The soft summer of the beginning will turn into the executioner that will test your life; it will take you to your limits and beyond.

You'll feel the excruciating heat of doubt, jealousy, treason, fear, impotence and dread of my presence.

You'll feel that this wrings out your soul, time and time again; it will mentally dismember you, it will blind you with its light; it will submerge you in the

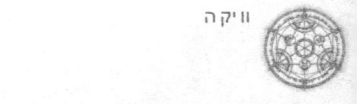

ויקה

A burning sands of desperation without having a balm; there isn't a drop that will calm your thirst.

Those will be difficult days that will test your mettle; during your life, you'll live many summers where happiness turns into pain and tragedy.

I'll be there during your summers, with my sisters; your destiny will be tested, your freedom, your inner strength, your wisdom, your determination and tenacity to live; they'll be subjected to the difficult test, time and time again, until you learn to get over your summers.

Once you've surrendered, and feel like all your strength has left you, then the summer gives up its impetuosity... It isn't a breather, it is the time for you to see your wounds, and understand that you have the power to heal and exceed.

Now, everything in your life, feelings, love, wealth or poverty, illusions, and dreams; everything you thought to be joy and happiness, in an instant, is now turned into ashes.

AUTUMN OF DEATH

The nostalgic days of autumn, where ashes and dead leaves are taken to their grave make their appearance.

The wind arrives along with the cry of life; it is the balm that relieves an aching heart. Autumn comes, you'll feel weak without illusions or dreams; empty, sad and nostalgic, you watch the days go by, locked in your sorrow, looking at a calendar already gone; and with it, many illusions died too.

You suffer, and your pain tends to wish for death; you'll invoke me many times in your life, more than you imagine; you'll wish deeply to die to avoid the torments of your summer.

You'll feel, deep inside you, that you can't take the agony and the pain anymore; no matter how it is disguised, a separation, a death, an economic loss, a betrayal, a deception or a disease; you can't even imagine how many disguises the Moirai can use.

But... It's over, now comes the time for acceptance, grief, and loneliness; just like the trees, who loose their leaves, your soul is freed; you start to accept, and you, slowly, get up.

Gradually, the new seeds will arrive, to sow the renovation of new illusions in your spirit; failed dreams disappear, allowing for new ones to grow in your soul.

Without knowing, the power of life after death will make you renew the fight to exist, waking up, without noticing, the strength of your soul. The seeds will be sowed, without knowing; you are focused on your mourning; in asking yourself, a thousand times, Why? You'll blame yourself another few times; you won't find answers and will ignore the secret of the What for? In your future, you'll probably be grateful when you learn the reasons, and of what you were freed from, and even of what you were saved from. The autumn of your life cleanses you, it takes the waste away, leaving a great wisdom in your soul; you've acquired and freed from yourself unlimited knowledge; you are free to decide if, in life, you live or die trapped in your pain.

WINTER OF DEATH

Winters come without warning, when you've caressed loneliness and your soul doesn't weep anymore; you are frozen, you want nothing, you wish for nothing, you are afraid to move on; you've entered the grief of the soul.

Nothing fills you, nothing gives you, you ignore that you've overcome your pain, and within you new illusions, and hopes, are created each morning.

The cold of the absence consumes you, the weight of adversity becomes lighter, somehow you understand; you continue, in spite of the pain; you slowly recover; very slowly...

In the measure of your suffering, where the concept of just or unjust is a torment, you can't even see that the mutation has only changed your destiny.

Something has died but, at the same time, something is born; only, you won't see that now, but is nestled in you; is in you, the seed that will give new fruit in a few days, when your loneliness is more intense, when you considered everything is lost, when you feel the abandonment and all you see is darkness.

When doubt consumes your soul, the pain has accumulated and the love has vanished with the

CHARLAS CON LA MUERTE

מדבר עם המוות

rainbow; when you feel that everything has died, you'll live again... You'll have the power... The strength of the life that makes its way from the afterlife. You'll feel the power in your soul, discover the new suns; if you really want it, if you allow me to brake the ice, in no time... Your winter, the coldest of winters, will die...

In a while... In a time without days or minutes, in any place; in a corner, in the solitude; wherever you least expected, a minute flower will grow; a soft ray of sun will tell you that your spring has began,

Me, death. I am your life.

Learn to recognize their signs when the seasons appear in cycles, in the path of your life; you'll be able to do it when you contemplate your life, each day, when you evaluate what you've done, and when you discover what you didn't.

Don't be afraid of my presence; let's make a pact of life where my shadows, along with my sisters, will make the path of life more bearable.

ויקה

Since the beginning of time, along with the shadows, and my sisters, the Moirai have answered the call to take care of destines; once invoked, they come; they are beings that value life, who seek pacts, those that have the power to act; the chosen ones are those who look into the future, who live intensely each day.

The pacts are intertwined, you live fully and we take care of your existence; you push yourself, and we open your paths; you turn your dreams into reality, and we'll erase each obstacle in your way.

Your life is so valuable, that you can't even imagine it; if you do one part, will do the rest, but... You must show your power, your strength your greatness; the difficulties and adversities that come into your life, only make you better, they train you, they turn you into a the living force of creation.

There is something you must do while you're alive, live! Push yourself to be happy, allow us to ease the path of your life, but... It's your freedom, if you see death as the end, and don't live, once you die you'll realize that I am life.

CHARLAS CON LA MUERTE

מדבר עם המוות

You'll regret that you left things undone; if you give me your hand, my sisters and I will give you ours, and when you die, you'll understand the secrets of life in your future incarnations.

This isn't the only life, there is infinite incarnations; if you live fully, if you waste this life, you'll live an eternity in the darkness; it is just up to you. Our pact is one of life, provided that you value each second of yours.

Not everyone can experience this encounter and continue in the world of opportunities; from now on, and while you live, spread the value of life in the world; you've entered and exited my domains; show and teach how lives are better when you understand death.

You have the freedom to open new paths of destiny where my sisters and I will be ready for anyone seeking our guidance, a pact with us will transcend in the eternities.

Don't impose or force; just show our path; whoever answers the call and invokes us, we'll be there; my sisters and I will stand up for your destiny, we'll

ויקה

ease the path, but... It's your freedom, sow the seed, do what you should do and don't stop doing it.

How do you live and how would you like to live?

Life is framed in destiny, and destiny depends on your decisions; but there is the mysterious and magical power, not just of death, but also of the energies that take care and protect the destinies.

Death and the Moirai, owners of fate, are energies; they act if you invoke them.

In the transit of life, there are difficult, sad, and joyful moments; the ideal is to have a life with the least setbacks as possible. That is when magic and luck come to play, allowing the destinies to be full, to be lucky and act; without a doubt, that is a path that leads to happiness.

One day, it will come; the way to unify oneself with that mysterious entity is transcribed in the ancient texts about death.

In fact, those who have made these pacts are able to have luck, happiness, well-being and success in their lives.

Why a pact gives results?

There is the collective conscience, just as the collective psychic energies; a representation of nature; let's take, for instance: the mango tree, which gives a seed; it is sowed and it gives more fruit, or mangoes, which will multiply through time forming a collective mango that was produced from a single seed.

The same happens with luck; groups of people with good luck; groups of people with bad luck; families suffering with curses for generations, and families that are blessed for generations. As we can see, it is an event of collective energies produced from one seed, or from a person who infects the rest.

It is the same with luck and success, radiated energies multiply, they can be appreciated in the different depressed areas of the big cities, or in the more prosper areas.

It is the same with thermites; only one produces so many that can destroy a house; or a mustard seed, only one produces millions. The pact with death is one seed that acts in the energy of whom makes and shares it; the gratitude returned is the Luck that radiates.

Just as it happens when you meet someone, whose life is changed, taking them form darkness to light; in no time you can evidence the presence of luck and happiness.

Now, this pact consists in sowing a seed, and receiving the energy of death, which, as we've said, is life. Death has been feared, cursed, condemned, but never destroyed; when you make a pact with death, you make a pact with life; this opens the doors so fortune, luck, and well-being come into your life. There are four sisters, Death and the three Moirai owners of destiny...

What they wish the most is for you to live, **BUT LIVE WELL!** No one is born to be unhappy.

CHARLAS CON LA MUERTE

מדבר עם המוות

This pact consists in sowing a seed in three different persons; each one will receive a book, just like this one, with the intension of one of the three Moirai.

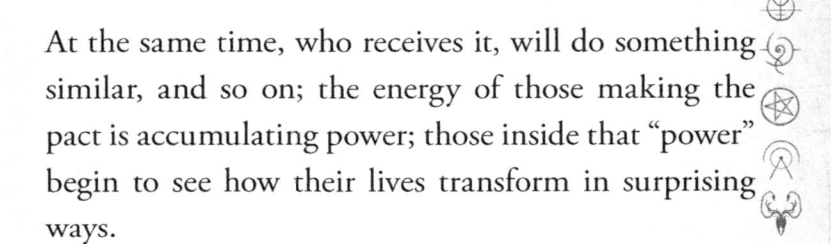

At the same time, who receives it, will do something similar, and so on; the energy of those making the pact is accumulating power; those inside that "power" begin to see how their lives transform in surprising ways.

Just as if you buy shares from a great company that progress, everyone progresses; you are doing the same in the enterprise of life. That is how energy of collective power is produced; it is your freedom, also when you die, what will prevail is "**What you left undone, when you had the chance to do it, but didn't**"...

Without a doubt, in magic, there are infinite rituals, amulets, talismans, and individual use potions, but few collective pacts like this one.

This book has fallen into your hands, for a reason, the magical stamp that comes with it is an amulet of power, which must activate once the pact with death is made; the key changes destinies, and opens the doors to a better life.

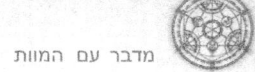

It will not happen if you don't act, also, it will not activate if you don't make the pact; please avoid making petitions if you don't make it; remember that the energies are moved by your intentions.

You receive one book and deliver three; by doing so, the collective magical sequence of events begins drawing luck and fortune. The energy generated is multiplied between everyone, and for everyone; at the same time, this creates a psychic field of protection; slowly, if you act in your life and practice what you've read, you'll perceive how your life acquires a different vibration.

The freedom is yours...

CHARLAS CON LA MUERTE

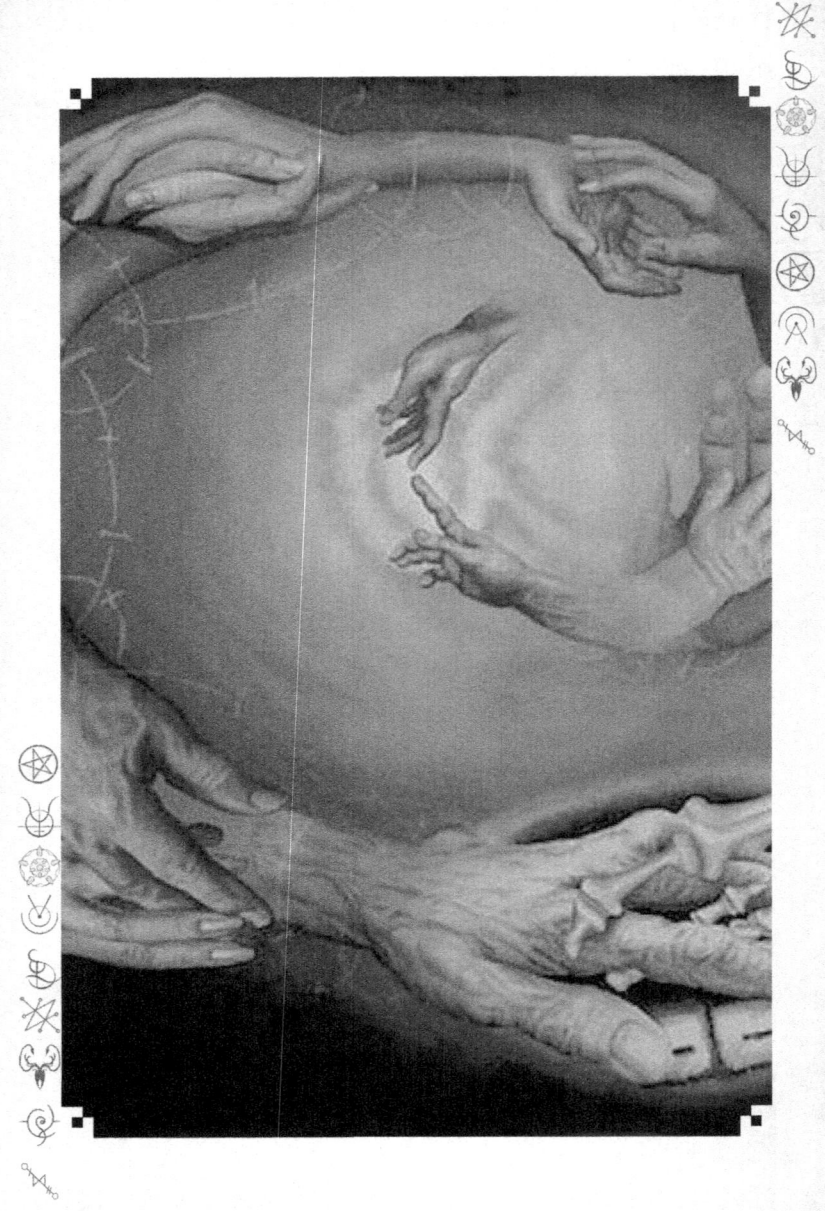

מדבר עם המוות

PACT WITH DEATH

It is actually a pact with life, the Moirai rule your destiny and your luck, before these generations, in the first cultures, and the souls knew the secrets of death.

I propose you become a sower of life, in return, I offer a pact; you promote life and, my sisters and I, protect yours; and you'll have a full life, without setbacks; you'll discover the beings who take care of your destiny, you'll see luck flow, fortune will come so you can have life and, when the time comes for your death, you'll see life and what you left in it; you now know what you must do for your future incarnations.

All souls are intertwined, those that are left after you leave, as well as the ones that incarnate in the future.

No one, beside us, knows the threads of destiny and luck; you want a full life, without setbacks, full of happiness. By making this pact, on the day of your departure, you'll have already known me; your next incarnation will be filled of gratitude energies of those who have valued life...

מדבר עם המוות

To propagate the devotion of the death you'll be facing is it to make an alliance of life. If you are not willing to make an offering in your benefit, and that of others; if you can't give if the true sense to your existence and push yourself to be better, don't try to make this pact; the day of your judgment you'll understand that the most important thing is what you left undone, when you had the chance to do it.

If this document, somehow, touched your soul, make the pact; if not, return this document to life; leave it somewhere, abandoned; another soul might appreciate it.

You don't take anything else from this world other than the knowledge extracted and the footprints you leave; this pact is to leave a footprint that will last for the duration of the souls; we've forgotten the true meaning of death; we try to live without so many barriers and setbacks, but we hold on to the worldly; death is inevitable, one day, it will come, and just as it was left in Greek and Egyptian cultures, the sacred symbols are, a pact with death; it is the pact of life.

You must pay for this pact; it's a universal law; something for something. What would you be willing to give?

ויקה

If you want a pact with death, choose one:

☠ **DEATH FOR DEATH:** If you make the pact death for death; one life in exchange for another; your firstborn, and firstborn descendants; but I won't tell you when I will collect; one year, or many.

☠ **LIFE FOR LIFE:** I give you life, but you must give your life; you'll take upon yourself the lives of those in pain; for the rest of your life, you'll be in charge of their responsibilities.

☠ **PAYMENT FOR PAYMENT:** You'll have to return everything you receive, and you'll receive what you give.

☠ **A SACRIFICE:** The sacrifice is to renounce to that you love; once you have it, you'll loose it; you'll sacrifice your love.

☠ **AN OFFERING:** Return three books, exactly like this one, where I dictate the secrets of life to you; it contains the three powers, the three symbols, the three fates, the three sacred magic, and the three vibrations of life.

With each book you give, the person making the pact, will have to sign with their name and keep it to open the whisper of death that will guide you thru adversity. I've given you the secret of life.

CHARLAS CON LA MUERTE

מדבר עם המוות

You want to live fully; each offering is a seed from the eternal tree; if you do it, read this book three times, and if you can discover the arcana that are in it, you'll see how your life open up like a flower in spring.

The sacred triquetta are three powers, that join past, present and future; birth, life and death; happiness, fortune and luck.

The three symbols that open and close the three doors of life. You must do this, when you give the three books to three different people...

First, sign your book... with your name, if you can, place a drop of blood; this is the book of your pact, and you have to keep it.

ויקה

> Today, I make a pact with death so, while I live, my life will be protected and I find the path to happiness...

YOUR NAME HERE

Second, keep in mind what you must do; when invoking the pact with death, you must deliver three equal books, to three different people so the power can multiply.

Each one represents one of the Moirai who control luck and destiny; the three will help your destiny and death will free you from sorrow. I must be clear, that this book can't be copied, or photocopied, or photographed by any means; if you do this the pact will reverse; in your conscience you'll know that you are doing wrong, so no good will come to you.

Once you do, in your mind you must pronounce, the prayer of every Moira to the book you are about to give, so, for each person who discovers life, gratitude will come to you in return; you'll se how the Moirai and Death your life shall protect.

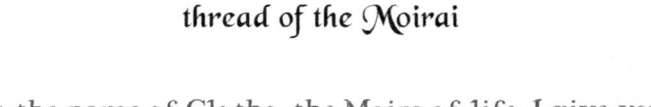

First book: (First person) Delivery of the first thread of the Moirai

In the name of Clotho, the Moira of life, I give you this book, so the doors of your life will open to the path of luck and happiness; so your days are blessed and your strength to exist is renewed.

With the profound love of existence, I sow the life in the life of this offering, with vows for your happiness.

This stamp with the sacred symbols is in your hands, as a sign of union, so our souls always remain united, that way adversity shall never come; like leaves from a tree, this seed sowed today shall forever grow.

Second book: (Second person) Delivery of the second thread of the Moirai

In the name of Lachesis, I make this offering to you, I know you need it, and with love for your soul I do it with devotion.

You need luck for your destiny to be different, where well-being reins, I beg the sister of death, that she can bring you all the luck, keeping you away from all the danger that can happen in life, attracting loves that will bring you happiness; if you read this book three times, don't doubt that your life shall change.

This stamp with the sacred symbols is in your hands, as a sign of union, so our souls always remain united, that way adversity shall never come; like leaves from a tree, this seed sowed today shall forever grow.

Third book: (Third person) Delivery of the third thread of the Moirai

In the name of Atropos, I make this offering to you, keeping a promise for a pact with life; I deliver it to you with pureness in my heart.

I know you need it to change yours and find the path where you find peace and healing.

I give you the wish for your upcoming days, luck is your companion, for bad days to stay away from you; so you find in your soul the power to follow the path and live again.

This stamp with the sacred symbols is in your hands, as a sign of union, so our souls always remain united, that way adversity shall never come; like leaves from a tree, this seed sowed today shall forever grow.

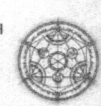

At the end, you'll do this...

I have fulfilled the offering, to help, many souls their life to change; I've spread the devotion of death to whom one day I will have to see, when my days end with her I'll be.

In her promise, my life, I'll live and since today, another life will be reborn, I leave the past dead, to begin again, having clear to value the precepts of life. I make a pact with death, to live fully and overcome adversity.

To fill myself with life, and leave something behind, for upcoming souls that thru their children will incarnate. I am part of life, death I will not fear, because her hand guides me, and I will be able to live.

When the end of my days is near, in my judgment I will see how many souls I've given life to, with this sacred pact I've made today and my life I will live.

CHARLAS CON LA MUERTE

מדבר עם המוות

This pact isn't of death or evil, it is of eternal life for incarnations; the doors of luck are opened, that gates of happiness, with the shining sun your wishes will be granted. When your day comes, and you are able to see, you left life and without a doubt you had nothing left to do...

After this pact, so we are united, I leave you the whisper of death as a legacy; in it, you can maybe find a beacon to guide you in the haze that will appear in your destiny. When you are faced with a problem of a difficulty, open any random page and you'll find wisdom.

Thru the different rituals in the world of magic, to increase the power of the pact of death, we suggest: these can only be done once the pact is made.

☠ To light the "***Candles of the Moirai***" that rule the destinies.

☠ Tuesday night, the candle of Clotho the spinner of destinies, to attract soul mates.

☠ Thursday at midnight, to torch the candle of Lachesis the Moira of luck.

☠ Saturday at sundown, Atropos, the Moira who prolongs or reduces life.

ויקה

This can be performed every time you wish to obtain a benefit; you must have the sacred potions and the coin, "***Charon's obol***". Also, you must draw the death symbols with the "***Sands of the souls***".

To invoke the Holly Death is to invoke life; **the next sacred stamp of Death**, we recommend you cut the page and keep it to perform the different rituals. This will unite you with the pact; millions of people will do the same.

Stay away from yourself, look into your heart, maybe you are responsible for what is causing your pain today.

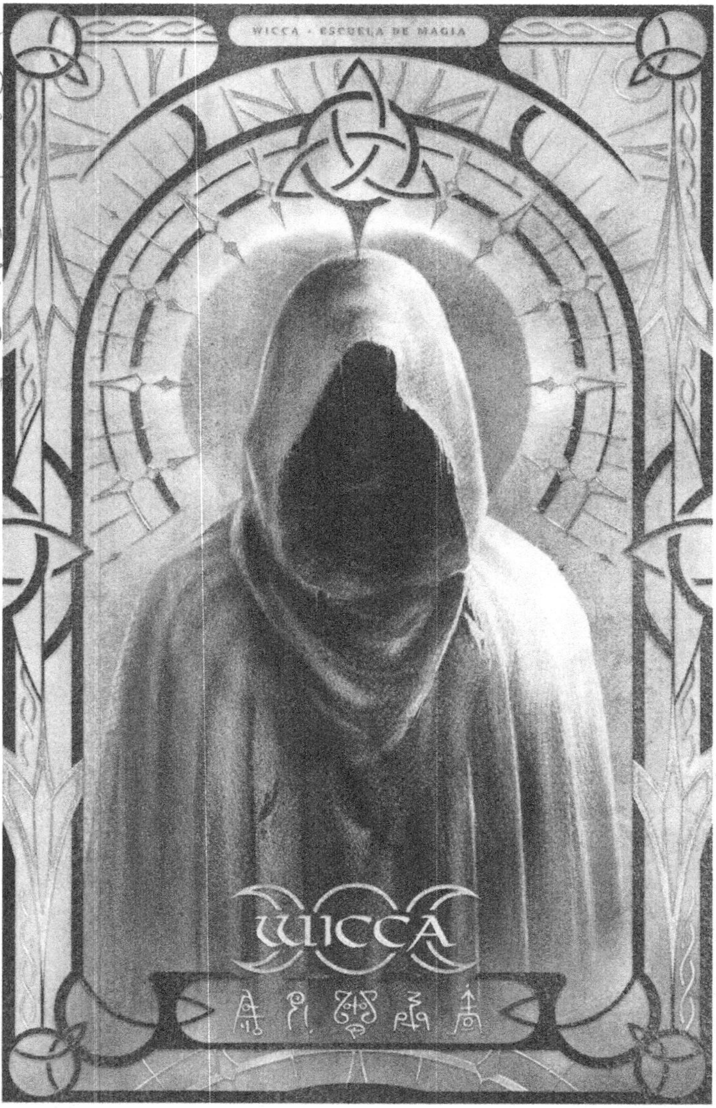
WICCA · ESCUELA DE MAGIA
WICCA

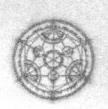

CHARLAS CON LA MUERTE

מדבר עם המוות

ויקה

THE WHISPER OF DEATH

Allow the sorrow to pass, think of starting over.

Don't break down son easily, you have the power to start; overcome your fears, you can do it.

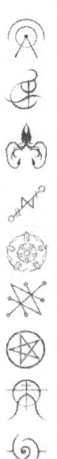

Don't do it...

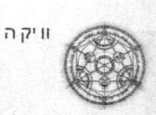

Look for the sincerity of your soul, you have something to mend; life only tells you to put your affairs in peace.

If you let your stubbornness win, you'll only have pain; things happen for a reason, don't fall in grief.

OMAR HEJEILE CH.

מדבר עם המוות

ויקה

205

CHARLAS CON LA MUERTE

מדבר עם המוות

Let the days go by You'll find another solution;
the Moira of luck will visit you, and calm your soul
down so you can wait for her...

מדבר עם המוות

What are you afraid of? It is time to face your fears, fight for your freedom, nothing is keeping you form it, you just have to choose what you want from your life, don't let yourself succumb...

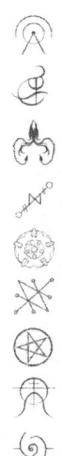

ויקה

Your destiny is not written, but you can write it; look at what you do, it is something you must choose, think on the future, you'll be able with this; wait a while and you'll be able to see everything more clearly.

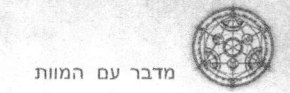

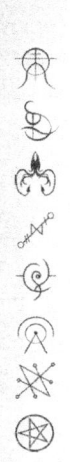

If you travel to the darkness, without light and guidance, you won't avoid your loss.

If you don't stay away from evil on time, without a doubt evil will trap you, and when it does, no one will be able to help you.

מדבר עם המוות

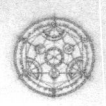

Don't leave anything pending, push yourself to make sure you have joy and happiness; if you ignore your tasks, think on what type of old age you'll have. How do you want to get to I, if you let yourself get old?

What are you sorry for, there is no gain in crying, what is done is done and can't be erased...

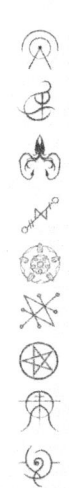

Don't let the past nestle in your present; it's not worth it... let it go...

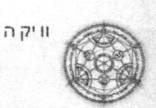

Freedom is yours, then why do you accept chains and yokes?

מדבר עם המוות

Make the pact with death; it'll be very helpful...

מדבר עם המוות

Your future is now...

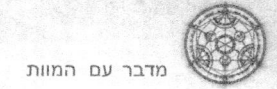

If you don't understand pain, why do you cause it?
Fix the damage you've done Before it is too late...

CHARLAS CON LA MUERTE

מדבר עם המוות

Nothing happens by chance, everything has a mysterious reason, watch carefully, the answers are in your heart.

ויקה

Look at your soul and think about your acts when adversity comes. You have to make payment for payment, revenge or justice, balance is natural; what you've done, it'll be done to you; there is no regret or forgiveness, much less malice; only the return; not even god will be able to change your life, not with prayers or pleas, could your soul be at peace; pay what you owe with an equal payment, but, sometimes, you'll have to pay more.

Payment for payment, you'll never be safe from that, and it will be the same in the other life; death will take care of that.

OMAR HEJEILE CH.

מדבר עם המוות

ויקה

The justice of life is in action; all of those who did me wrong are paying for it.

If you are dead today, your life has passed, your loved possessions have been left in the unfathomable yesterday; you left much to be done, you left your work unfinished, you left empty an opportunity to live; today that you understand the value of a life, the time you are wasting, today that you are so close, and so far, of the reality Today that you long for what you don't have, nor won't have; what would you do if I let you live...?

What would you offer death in exchange for another opportunity? Think hard before you answer; you either continue your way to another incarnation, or you go back and finish your work.

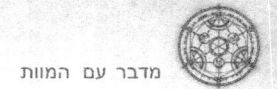

Today you have something to be grateful for...

CHARLAS CON LA MUERTE

מדבר עם המוות

If you challenge destiny, you'll have to deal with what it'll bring you...

ויקה

מדבר עם המוות

ויקה

Don't you dare interrupting other destinies, be silent and think before you talk; what ever you say you won't be able to erase.

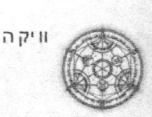

The fear for the future, is the best fear; that'll help you not to make mistakes; think hard on what you do, and what you are going to do...

No one can judge you, nothing can condemn you; you only know what you do, and why you do it.

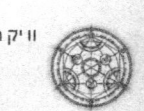

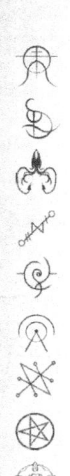

Maybe no one knows what you live and do; you know it, and you'll have to evaluate it in your judgment.

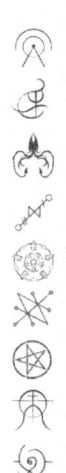

Be ware of the shadows, if you don't know how they can deceive you, don't trust who praises you; they are working on a plot to do harm.

מדבר עם המוות

ויקה

Don't venture in the unknown, unless you know how to get out.

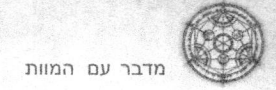

Today is your tomorrow; yesterday doesn't count...

CHARLAS CON LA MUERTE

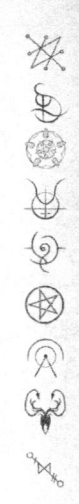

מדבר עם המוות

In each book you give, sow a seed for your future, not just the worldly; but a seed that will bloom thru your incarnations; death is the eternal life.

ויקה

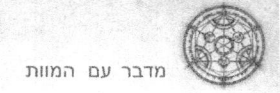

Where are you going? How sure are you to know what is right...

Chance is not the solution to your life; study, work, build and don't stop.

OMAR HEJEILE CH.

מדבר עם המוות

ויקה

Your relatives are not your family...

Don't deprive yourself from living and enjoying,
"Live"

No one can deceive you; you deceive yourself.

You'll never recover lost time.

No one can do you harm, you allow it.

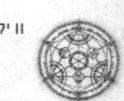

מדבר עם המוות

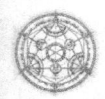

ויקה

If you judge the same thing you do, who must be the condemned?

Stop Think well if it is really what you want; if you begin your destiny in the darkness, you hardly return to the light.

מדבר עם המוות

Don't be afraid Be brave.

Speak, don't be quiet; let out the venom that consumes you And be prepared...

If you have no dignity, what's the use of fighting?

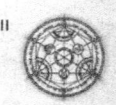

מדבר עם המוות

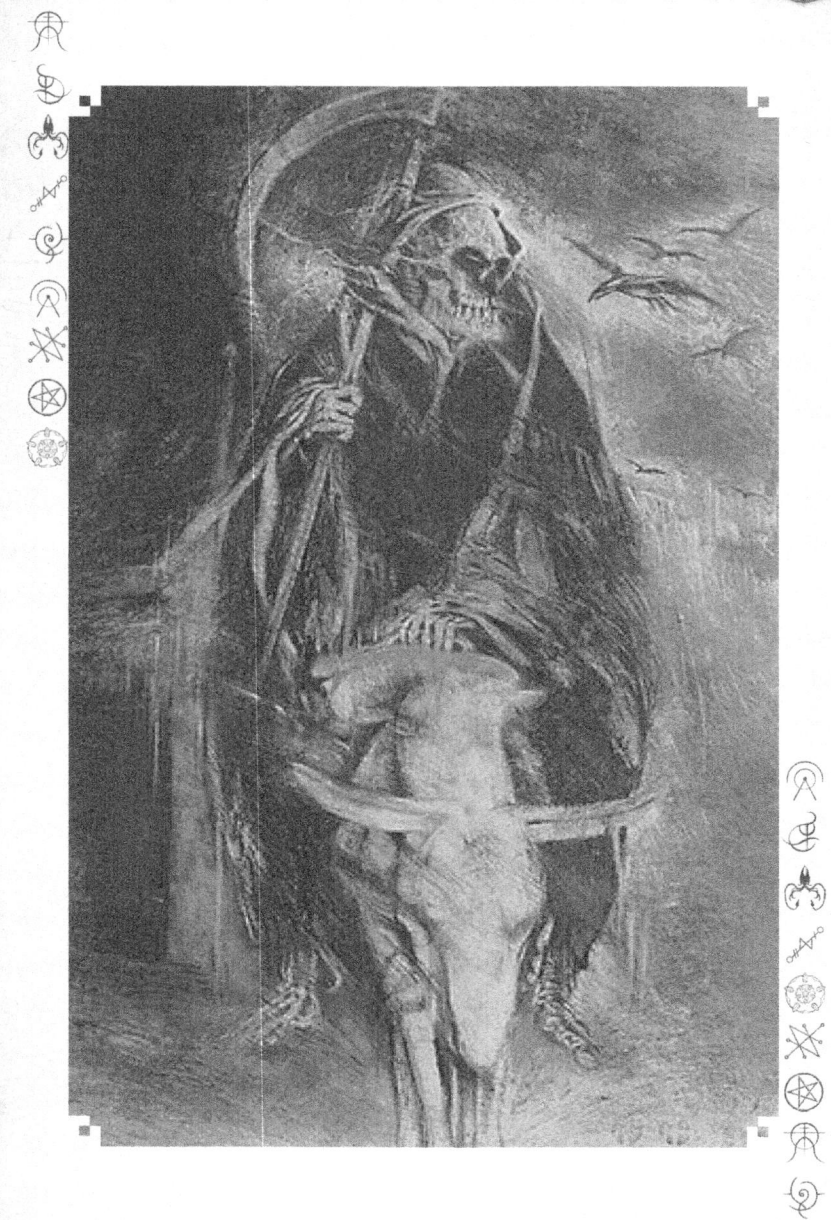

No one can humiliate you; you do it on your own.

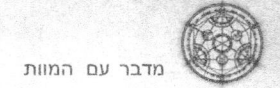

Love is not possessing, let it free...

CHARLAS CON LA MUERTE

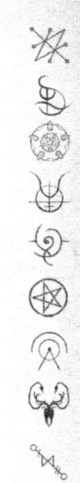

מדבר עם המוות

You've made a mistake... fix it¡

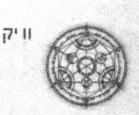

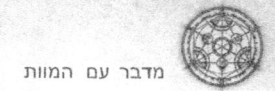

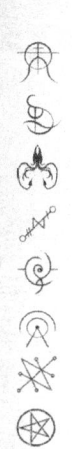

Nothing dies; death is the beginning of something new. Wait for it¡

Problems are just hidden solutions; normally, you'll find them without looking.

OMAR HEJEILE CH.

מדבר עם המוות

ויקה

Don't interfere in other destinies that aren't your own.

Learn to say No¡

If you want something, you must give something

Don't fear absences, they are the balm that heals the souls.

There are things in life that you can do nothing against, accept them¡

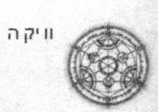

You never loose, never win; it is just the cycle of life

The truth doesn't exist.

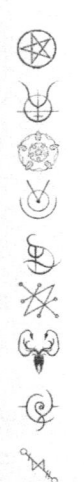

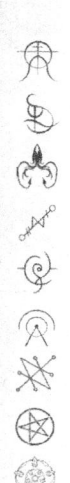

Everything is yours, but you won't be able to have anything, so forget.

.... Death got silent... I was taken to other worlds that exist between life and death; when I felt the haze, I understood that death is life. We live without knowing the profound content of being incarnated; in the same freedom, there is the concept that there is nothing after life, just a dream from which you don't wake up, but... There is another reality, the continuity of the souls.

Nothing disappears forever in nature, there is no way it can be done; no matter how much you try to destroy anything, the only thing you do is transform it; it dies in one state to be another.

The butterfly is born and dies many times before becoming a butterfly; all nature renews itself to die, and dies to live. It is the mind that ignores such profound wisdom about the lives and deaths that are, in themselves, life and death.

By understanding that the incarnated essence doesn't disappear, the incarnation makes sense; when one observes that the new arriving souls have memories from other lives, not from places or persons, but memories of profound knowledge.

Thanatonauts or travelers of death, which science identify as the Lazarus syndrome; the spontaneous return of those who have died and come back to life.

They narrate the out-of-body experiences they've had while being dead; ancient monks, in deep concentration, lived another type of out-of-body experiences known as unfolding.

Phisionomicaly, bodes are similar, the same organs, the same physiological processes in all of them, but... Are so different in personalities, even among siblings, biological children of the same essence; same eggs, same sperm, similar bodies, but profoundly different.

The soul is the being that vibrates along with the spirit and the earthly world; it is the conscience of being when you read these lines, the voice in your mind, and the questions or affirmations it makes, are projections of your soul.

That is the energy that separates from the death, and occasionally, escapes with the dreams; in your mind, there are events that you now remember, from episodes, from dreams or states of lethargy, where

CHARLAS CON LA MUERTE

מדבר עם המוות

you have felt outside of your body. It is the fantastic energy of life, controlled by death; it incarnates and disincarnates thru the infinity of time and space.

If you are in a state of relaxation, you'll enter your mind, traveling to your deepest memories, and you'll be able to see your soul. Your wishes, that which you like and are passionate about; that mysterious something that makes you feel a profound attraction for something in particular; your tastes are not from this world, they are memories captured in your spirit; something from other incarnations.

There is no human way to demonstrate life after death, but there are countless phenomena that allow us to explain that something extraordinary happens before dying.

- Recovering radiated energy or collecting steps.
- Detachment of ties or bonds with close people, movement of objects, dreams and premonitions.
- The arm of death, feelings of spontaneous paralysis when in a conscious state.
- Illness or death of a pet
- Appearance of certain birds or insects.

ויקה

- Perception of scents, the smell of wet dirt, flowers, incense, etc.
- Behaviors performed by some people before they die: organize, sew, clean, repair, talk about death, etc.
- Premonitions of death; it is the sensation that manifests like pressure on the chest, prevents serenity and produces a feeling of uneasy for days, before someone close dies; after their death, the feeling disappears.
- Premonitory dreams announcing that someone is going to die; normally, it begins with a revealing dream that repeats when someone is going to die.
- Heaviness in the environments.
- Hypothermia, or a feeling of extreme cold.
- Apparition of strange lights or small fires.
- Apparition of light spheres, gauze, or frost.

There are several signs that can be perceived before death; if there was no detachment, they should not take place; and if they take place, that "energy" must migrate somewhere.

After the death

- Invisible presences
- Scents identifying the deceased person
- Appearance of the ghost, gauze with the shape of the deceased person
- Appearance of specters; one can see the silhouette of the person, but in their decomposition state; it, normally, appears like that to the people they caused harm.
- A vision of the soul; a shapeless intense light that appears.
- Revealing dreams
- Sounds
- Psychophonies that can be recorded, voices from the deceased person.
- Movement of objects

There are several phenomena that appear after a death which to the point of possessed homes; where no one can live. All these elements, and many more, can open a window that helps to understand that there is some kind of continuity after death. It isn't hard to find, thru the history of mankind, the most profound treaties about death; Greeks, Egyptians, Mayans;

practically every culture, religion, and creed, have confirmed the presence of death and its mysteries.

In one way or the other, it is a topic that exists latent in every mind; death is an inevitable event of life. Talks with Death is a personal experience; at no time I intend to convince anyone of the existence of another life, but...

You are free to accept this book for your life, or ignore it, I'm just transcribing an event; if you consider that this document has served you well, and wish a pact of life; you are free to do so.

But... You must always think what is important, what you've done, or what you left undone?

Everything you live today is temporary; your soul discovers the true meaning of life in the difficulties... Test yourself...

The only thing that time doesn't forgive is what isn't done on time... Someday, your phase will be...

Am I Dead?

CHARLAS CON LA MUERTE

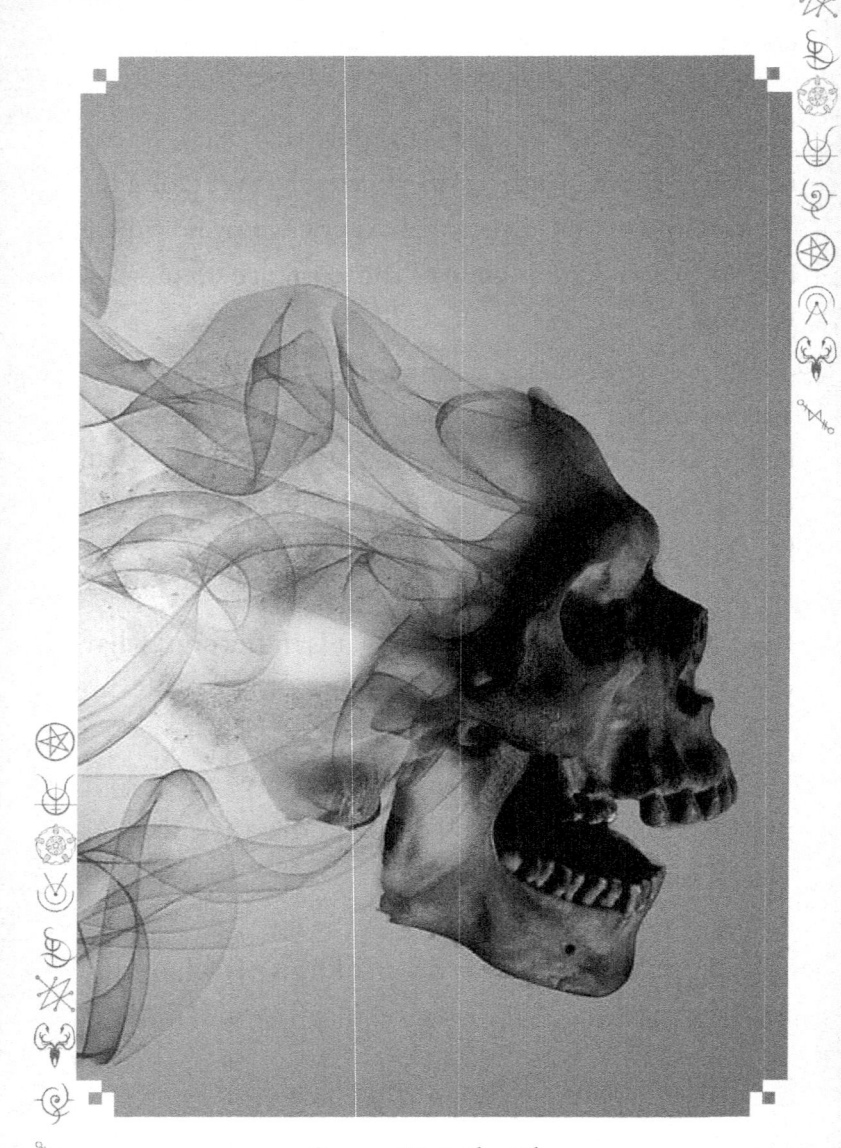

מדבר עם המוות

Omar Hejeile Ch.

Encyclopedia Universe of Magic

Want to learn magic?

Enter the school of magic thru our encyclopedia in Ofiuco Wicca. The hidden power of the mind, the influence without space or time. Knowledge kept for millennia, now at your hands.

OPHIUCHUS

WWW.OPHIUCHUS.US

Made in the USA
Middletown, DE
03 January 2023